FIRST BELONG TO
GOD

ON RETREAT
with
POPE FRANCIS

AUSTEN IVEREIGH

Foreword by Pope Francis

T0049631

LOYOLAPRESS.
A JESUIT MINISTRY

Chicago

LOYOLA PRESS.
A JESUIT MINISTRY

www.loyolapress.com

Scripture quotations are from the *New Revised Standard Version Bible: Catholic Edition*, copyright © 1989, 1993 National Council of the Churches of Christ in the United States of America. Used by permission. All rights reserved worldwide.

Cover art credit: neneo/Shutterstock, Katsumi Murouchi/Moment/Getty Images
Back cover author photo: Divisione Produzione Fotografica/VaticanMedia

ISBN: 978-0-8294-5791-9
Library of Congress Control Number: 2023949053

Printed in the United States of America.
23 24 25 26 27 28 29 30 31 32 SMN Bang 10 9 8 7 6 5 4 3 2 1

FIRST BELONG TO
GOD

For Diego Fares, SJ,
in memoriam.

Other Books by Austen Ivereigh

The Great Reformer

Wounded Shepherd

and,
co-authored with Pope Francis,
Let Us Dream: The Path to a Better Future.

Contents

Foreword by Pope Francis xi

Introduction xv

Note on Acronyms xxi

Day One   Wonderfully Made 1

Day Two   To Come Out from Ourselves 21

Day Three The Lord of the World 45

Day Four   Called, Chosen, Sent 65

Day Five   The Ecology of Mercy 87

Day Six   Around the Common Table 111

Day Seven The Triumph of Failure 135

Day Eight A New Imagination of the Possible 157

A User Guide 179

Overview of the Retreat 182

Leaving the Exercises 185

Sources 189

Bibliography 207

Acknowledgments 211

About the Author 213

Foreword

by Pope Francis

Precisely because of his life experience, St. Ignatius of Loyola saw with great clarity that every Christian is involved in a battle that defines his or her life. It is a struggle to overcome the temptation of closing in on ourselves, so that the love of the Father can make its home in us. When we make room for the Lord who rescues us from our self-sufficiency, we open up to all of creation and every creature. We become channels of the Father's life and love. Only then do we realize what life truly is: a gift of the Father who loves us deeply and desires that we belong to him and to each other.

This battle has already been won for us by Jesus through his ignominious death on the Cross and his Resurrection. In this way, the Father revealed definitively and for all time that his love is stronger than all the powers of this world. But even so it remains a struggle to embrace and make real that victory: We continue to be tempted to close ourselves to that grace, to live in a worldly way, in the illusion that we are sovereign and self-sufficient. All the life-threatening crises that beset us around the world, from the ecological crisis to the wars, the injustices against the poor and vulnerable, have their roots in this rejection of our belonging to God and to each other.

The Church helps us in many ways to struggle against that temptation. Its traditions and teachings, its practices of prayer and confession and the regular celebration of the Eucharist are "channels of grace" that open us to receive the gifts that the Father wishes to pour out on us.

Among those traditions are spiritual retreats, and among those are the *Spiritual Exercises* of St. Ignatius of Loyola.

Because of the relentless pressures and tensions of an obsessively competitive society, retreats to "recharge our batteries" have become very popular. But a Christian retreat is very different from a "wellness" holiday. The center of attention is not us but God, the Good Shepherd, who, instead of treating us like machines, responds to our deepest needs as his beloved children.

The retreat is a time for the Creator to speak directly to his creatures, inflaming our souls with his "love and praise" so that we might "better serve God in the future," in the words of St. Ignatius (SE 15). Love and service: these are the two great themes of the *Spiritual Exercises*. Jesus comes out to meet us, breaking our chains that we might walk with him as his disciples and companions.

When I think of the fruits of the *Exercises*, I see Jesus saying to the paralytic by the pool of Beth-zatha: "Stand up, take your mat and walk!" (John 5:1–16). It is an order that needs to be obeyed and is, at the same time, his most gentle and loving invitation.

The man was internally paralyzed. He felt a failure in a world of rivals and competitors. Resentful and bitter at what he felt he had been denied, he was trapped in the logic of self-sufficiency, convinced that everything depended on him and his own strength. And as the others are stronger and faster than he is, he has fallen into despair. But it is there that Jesus came out to meet him with his mercy and calls him out of himself. Once he opens to Jesus' healing power, his paralysis, both inner and outer, is cured. He can get up to walk ahead, praising God and working for his Kingdom, freed from the myth of self-sufficiency and learning each day to depend more on his grace. In this way the man becomes a disciple, able to face better not only the challenges of this world, but also to challenge the world to operate according to the logic of gift and love.

As Pope, I have wanted to encourage our belonging "first" to God, and then to creation and to our fellow human beings, especially to those who cry out to us. This is why I have wanted to keep in view the two great crises of our age: the deterioration of our common home and the mass migration and displacement of people. Both are symptoms of the "crisis of non-belonging" described in these pages. For the same reason I have wanted to encourage the Church to rediscover the gift of its own tradition of synodality, for when it opens to the Spirit that speaks in the People of God, the whole Church gets up and walks ahead, praising God and helping to bring about his Kingdom.

I am glad to see these themes so present in *First Belong to God*, tied to the contemplations of St. Ignatius that have shaped me over the years. Austen Ivereigh has done a great service in bringing together the retreat talks I gave many decades ago with my teachings as Pope. In this way, he allows both to illuminate, and be illuminated by, St. Ignatius's *Spiritual Exercises*.

This is not a time to hunker down and lock our doors. I see clearly that the Lord is calling us out of ourselves, to get up and walk. He asks us not to turn away from the pains and cries of our age, but to enter into them, opening channels of his grace. Each of us is that channel by virtue of our baptism. The question is to open it and keep it open.

May these eight days of enjoying his love help you to hear the Lord's call to become a source of life, hope, and grace for others, and so discover the true joy of your life. May you find the *magis* that St. Ignatius speaks of, that "more," which calls us to discover the depths of God's love in the greater giving of ourselves.

And please, whenever you remember, don't forget to pray for me, that I may help us always belong first to God.

Franciscus

Vatican City, October 12, 2023
Feast Day of Mary of the Pillar

We are born, beloved creatures of our Creator,
God of love, into a world that has lived long before us.
We belong to God and to one another, and we are
part of creation. And from this understanding,
grasped by the heart, must flow our love for each other,
a love not earned or bought because all we are
and have is unearned gift.

—Pope Francis

Only on the basis of God's gift, freely accepted and
humbly received, can we cooperate by our own efforts in
our progressive transformation. We must first belong to
God, offering ourselves to him who was there first, and
entrusting to him our abilities, our efforts, our struggle
against evil, and our creativity, so that his free gift
may grow and develop within us.

—Pope Francis

Introduction

First Belong to God grew out of an eight-day *Spiritual Exercises* that I was asked to lead in July 2020 for the British Province of the Jesuits. We were due to meet at St. Beuno's, the Jesuit spirituality center in North Wales, but by then the UK, along with much of the world, was in and out of coronavirus pandemic lockdowns. With St. Beuno's closed to visitors, we went ahead anyway, online, dispersed in our gathering but linked by screens and fellowship and the vulnerability we were feeling at that time.

At that moment it was still not clear how bad it would get and how many might die. For the past three months it had felt as if humanity were being sifted; this was a hinge moment, a threshold. There were so many stories of death and loss and sadness, but also of courage and compassion and new insight. As Pope Francis had told us repeatedly over Easter 2020, a crisis was a time of choosing, and from a time of crisis like COVID, the choices would be decisive. You might come out of it better or worse, he said, but you couldn't come out the same.

It was a good moment, you might say, for a retreat.

Propitious, too, was the theme I had chosen long before the virus struck: the joy of belonging. It was the invitation Francis had been making throughout his pontificate, but felt now with a new urgency. COVID brought terrible, often fatal, isolation, when people felt invisible and hopeless. The suffering of our peripheries—migrant centers, prisons, elderly care homes—was brutal, and suddenly more visible. Institutions were pushed to the brink, and basics we took for granted suddenly scarce. But it was also a time to discover new kinds of belonging, as people looked out for one another, using technology to create networks of solidarity. We also reconnected with the created world and rediscovered our interior lives. Getting vaccinated and staying at home for the sake of the elderly and vulnerable reminded us that there is a common good that comes before our own interests. As an organizing principle, liberal individualism suddenly seemed not just inadequate but also criminally negligent.

It was as if humanity had been given a time of trial in order to test the very proposition of belonging, to awaken society to what had been forgotten. In his lockdown *Urbi et Orbi* homily on the night of March 27, 2020, when he spoke to the world from a dark, wet, St. Peter's Square, Francis put it memorably: "Amid this storm, the façade of those stereotypes with which we camouflaged our egos, always worrying about appearances, has fallen away, revealing once more the ineluctable and blessed awareness that we are part of one another, that we are brothers and sisters of one another."

At the time I gave the retreat for the Jesuits and their collaborators, I had begun to work with Francis on what would be, when it came out later that year, a special little book. *Let Us Dream: The Path to a Better Future* was intended for a broad readership without any particular spiritual formation. But it was packed with Francis's wisdom on how humanity could emerge better from the pandemic, born of insights into the way God's grace operates in times of tribulation. This had been something of a special topic for Jorge Mario Bergoglio since long before he became Pope. He had a unique capacity to navigate tempests and bring the boat safely into harbor. It was why the Jesuits in Argentina used to call him the "storm pilot." They must have smiled that night of the *Urbi et Orbi*, when Francis said we had been caught off guard by a sudden storm, and needed now to row together.

Let Us Dream showed Francis's reading of the moment: The pandemic was a lens through which we could view the many other pandemics humanity faces at this time. Whether the climate emergency, accelerating inequality and insecurity, vast populations on the move across borders, or the rise in authoritarian populism and national rivalries spilling over into war, ours is an extraordinarily turbulent age. The crises may not have a single cause, but it was clear that meeting the challenges they present would take more than new policies and technologies. Nothing less than a conversion in our way of seeing and way of being was called for.

What was lacking was that "blessed awareness that we are part of one another, that we are brothers and sisters of one another," as Francis explained in *Fratelli Tutti* (32). This could be understood only with a spiritual lens. For Francis, the key to our capacity to confront and grow through these crises is a threefold belonging: to God, to creation, and to one another. The loss of our sense of belonging to a single human family that is part of creation has its roots in closing ourselves off from our Creator. The result is that we are uniquely ill-prepared to manage the transition to a better future.

This crisis of nonbelonging is so well documented by sociologists and psychologists that it has become almost a cliché. Especially in the wealthy West, the statistics, whether on social exclusion, suicide among the young, the fall in the birthrate, or mental ill-health linked to a sense of alienation and "ontological homelessness," are sobering. In her book *On Belonging*, Kim Samuel writes of this as "an age of isolation" in which "much of humanity is grappling with myriad forms of alienation, disenfranchisement, and feelings of separation." Marriage and family, the workplace, culture—all are increasingly marked by what the late Zygmunt Bauman, a Polish-born sociologist and philosopher, who met and had great admiration for Francis, famously called "liquid modernity," in which precariousness in economic and social conditions lead men and women to perceive the world as a container full of disposable objects, objects for one-off use—including other human beings. Restless, anxious, and insecure, people find it hard to build community, seeking security in a common identity designed to keep the other, the stranger, at a distance. We are living in an age both of decomposing bonds and identity fundamentalism.

Francis has addressed this crisis of non-belonging at its roots. You can track the arc in his major teaching documents, as well as in, after 2017, his dialogues with Bauman, who told the Pope that he saw him as "the light at the end of the tunnel." The loss of belonging to a single human family that is part of creation is addressed in Francis's two "Franciscan" social encyclicals, *Laudato Si'*, "On the Care of Our Common Home" in 2015, and *Fratelli Tutti*, "On Fraternity and Social Friendship" in 2020. Before either of those was *Evangelii Gaudium*, "On the Proclamation of the Gospel in Today's World," which came out in his first year, 2013. Both there and in his short but powerful document on holiness, *Gaudete et Exsultate*, "On the Call to Holiness in Today's World" in 2018, Francis dealt comprehensively with the first and most important kind of belonging, to God our Creator and Father. In that first relationship of mutuality and reciprocity—the belonging we are born into—is what Christianity traditionally calls salvation: freedom and life for us, and for others. It is at the origin of the two other kinds of belonging.

This theme of triple belonging—to our Creator, to creation, and to our fellow creatures—is closely related to what Francis calls *salir de sí*, or "coming out of ourselves." His teaching has been organized to help us embrace this self-transcendence, and confront its contrary temptation to close in on ourselves in egotistical self-isolation and distrustful self-withholding. This is the lure of what he calls "self-immanence," the illusion of self-sufficiency or worldliness. In contemporary culture, this goes by various names—individualism, materialism, egotism—and is described by Francis in *Fratelli Tutti* when he speaks of loss of the sense of belonging to a single human family. "What reigns instead is a cool, comfortable and globalized indifference, born of deep disillusionment concealed behind a deceptive illusion: thinking that we are all-powerful, while failing to realize that we are all in the same boat" (FT 30).

For Francis what causes this tendency to isolation and focus on self-interest is not change per se. As with any age, changes in this one are a mix of good and bad, threat and opportunity. While he is deeply troubled by the social fragmentation of liquid modernity, he is not nostalgic for a previous era, and regards the desire to recover the past as a temptation that in Italian he calls *indietrismo*: a backwards-focus that keeps us locked in desolation. Rather, he recognizes that rapid changes and fragmentation trigger anxiety and fear, and with these comes the temptation to distrust God and close in on ourselves. That's what was happening on the boat in the storm in Mark's Gospel (see Mark 4:35–41), which Francis spoke of that night in March 2020 in St. Peter's Square.

To "come out of ourselves," then, is to resist these temptations and to recover our deeper belonging. In receiving God's mercy and in appreciating that all is gift, we open ourselves to new freedom and possibility. We allow the Spirit to guide us into a better future. We regenerate the bonds of our belonging. New life flows into our lives, and into our Church. This is the invitation of Francis's teaching, and the hoped-for grace of this retreat.

What follows is what I offered the Jesuits and their collaborators but expanded and updated. It follows the broad pattern of a traditional eight-day "preached" version of the month-long *Spiritual Exercises*, moving through Ignatius's signature meditations and contemplations. Days One, Two, and Three belong to the first "week"; Days Four through Six belong to the second "week"; Days Seven and Eight belong to the third and fourth "weeks". There are four reflections for each day and suggestions for prayer. How the material is structured as well as how it may be used—over longer periods, and in groups, for example—is set out in detail at the back, along with a summary framework, an Overview of the Retreat, which maps each day's themes and readings.

It is a "retreat with Pope Francis" not just in the sense that it is a way into his teachings but also because it quotes from retreat talks he gave as a Jesuit, and later, as cardinal. These talks, most of which have never been published in English, are a treasure trove and a reminder that, before he was elected the 264th successor of St. Peter, Jorge Mario Bergoglio was a formidable Ignatian spiritual director. It is a joy and privilege—if also an intimidating responsibility—to bottle up this fine wine and make it available to the wider Church.

The path to a better future, the future God desires for us, begins in the human heart, in our yearning to belong. In those desires is the road out of our crises, both our own and those of our world. By regenerating the bonds that bind us, in reoxygenating us to receive the gift that is our life and our world, we need first to know and experience the Giver, who is already here, waiting for us. There is no better manual for this than the *Spiritual Exercises* of Ignatius, and no greater spiritual guide in our time than Francis, the world's first Jesuit pope.

Having received so many gifts from both, my gift to you is to put you in their hands.

May this be a blessed time for you.

Note on Acronyms

Documents frequently referred to in these pages are referenced in the text by their acronyms, followed by the paragraph or section number in the case of papal teaching documents and the *Spiritual Exercises*, or the page number in the case of *Let Us Dream*. Thus (SE 140) refers to number 140 of the *Spiritual Exercises*, (LUD 89) refers to page 89 of *Let Us Dream*, and (EG 29) refers to paragraph 29 of *Evangelii Gaudium*.

The following acronyms for papal teachings are used in the text:

- AL = *Amoris Laetitia* (2016)
- DD = *Desiderio Desideravi* (2022)
- EG = *Evangelii Gaudium* (2013)
- FT = *Fratelli Tutti* (2020)
- GE = *Gaudete et Exsultate* (2018)
- LS = *Laudato Si'* (2015)
- QA = *Querida Amazonia* (2019)

Also included are the following:

- SE = *Spiritual Exercises of St. Ignatius*
- LUD = *Let Us Dream*

To avoid footnote numbers cluttering the page in addition to these references, information on other citations and references are given in the Sources section at the back of the book.

✝

The goal of our life is to live with God forever.

God, who loves us, gave us life.

Our own response to love allows God's life

to flow into us without limit . . . .

Our only desire and our one choice should be this:

I want and I choose what better leads

to God's deepening his life in me.

—St. Ignatius of Loyola

DAY ONE

Wonderfully Made

*On Understanding Ourselves as God-Belonging
Creatures, Made Out of Love for Love*

Created in Love

There is a moment, like this one at the start of our retreat, that
the monk writer Thomas Merton called *le point vierge*, the "virginal
point." It is the place of fresh possibility, the moment when things can
begin anew. Many of us know it when we stumble on some beauty,
truth, or goodness that opens a new horizon, or sense an inrush of
the Holy Spirit while in prayer, silence, or solitude. The virginal point
brings a joyful, expectant peace; it is to experience, in relief and joy,
our true self. It is the point from where we see "the innocence for
which we were created, which we have lost and which we can regain,"
in Merton's words.

This is grace, an irruption of the divine, that reveals to us both that
we were created and can again be re-created. Many words are spilled
to describe these moments, but they cannot match the experience. "I
am about to do a new thing," says the Lord in Isaiah. "Now it springs
forth, do you not perceive it?" (Isaiah 43:19a).

"The characteristic common to God and man is apparently . . . the
desire and ability to make things," observed writer Dorothy L. Sayers.
This capacity to make, humans have from God; creativity is one of
the ways we image our Creator. The first gift of our Creator is creation

1

itself, which we are handed at birth. "We are not God," says Pope Francis in *Laudato Si'*. "The earth was here before us and it has been given to us" (LS 67).

Because I have written this book, this book belongs to me (at least, in a different way than the way it belongs to you, who may have bought it or been given it). That might seem a strange claim when you think how much it depends on others: Pope Francis for its content; the publishers for editing it and laying it out and getting it into your hands; and you, for whom it was written. Yet as its *author*, I have *author*ity over it: in Latin, *auctor* and *auctoritas* denote an ownership that carries with it a particular responsibility.

Just as this book belongs to me because I created it, so, in a far more important and absolute way, do we belong to God who created us. In a lesser way, we belong to those people and places made by him that have also made and helped to form us. Many of them have had authority over and responsibility for us. As products of the places and people that preceded us—their gifts and hurts, their possibilities and limits—we are their creatures too.

"In the beginning when God created the heavens and the earth" is how it all starts (Genesis 1:1). Before the beginning was the *point vierge*, when the eternal God chose to love the universe into being, to create time and the seasons, the days and the nights. God is the great Maker, and we come to know God best through what he has made and in the act of making itself. Every time a creature is born or a new day breaks or we pause in prayer or we come on retreat, there is a virginal point we are called to attend to, and in the place of that new possibility we can find again the divine power that flows through the universe and in us, that creates and re-creates us.

We can study God; we can debate ideas and concepts of God, but we *know* God directly through experiencing his creation and his re-creation. When we take time to let God seek us out, as we do here now, we are opening ourselves to this virginal point. "God moves in our hearts to be experienced and then makes us all to be artists of the kingdom," as artist Makoto Fujimora puts it. When we told people we were *making* a retreat, did we grasp what that means?

We make a retreat to know our Maker. On a retreat we create space and time for our Creator to communicate with us, his creatures. The word *creation* means more than just "nature," says Francis in *Laudato Si'*, for in the Jewish-Christian tradition "it has to do with God's loving plan in which every creature has its own value and significance" (LS 76). We go on retreat to find, or perhaps discover afresh, God's plan in the design and purpose of his creation—which includes us.

So much thinking and spirituality today is disincarnate, even gnostic. People seek God outside and above creation, in abstraction and purity and complexity. But the creation story of Genesis, the Incarnation in Luke and Matthew, and the Cross in all the Gospels tell us that the reverse is true: in Francis's words, God is close and concrete. God creates this world as good and beautiful, wanting all his creatures to thrive. And the place we find God is right here, down here with his creatures, "in all things."

God made the world *ex nihilo* and *ex amore*, as the ancients put it. "Out of nothing" means that creation serves no need of God; he does not create us because he needs us. "Out of love" means that God created us because it is in God's nature to create, for the sake of creation itself. And so, like a great work of art or craft, we are "wonderfully made" (Psalm 139). As human creatures created *ex nihilo* and *ex amore*, each of us has an in-built significance, a deep value, and an inherent purpose; we are a means to no one's end, for we are created *out of* love, *for* love.

The distinction made in the Gospels and in St. Paul between "flesh" and "spirit" is not the dualistic distinction between material world and ethereal heaven but between creation and "new creation," creation created anew by the rising of Christ. To live by the spirit is not to flee our creaturehood but to participate in that new act of creation: in God's loving, nurturing, healing power, making us afresh.

In opening each of his creatures up to one another, God helps us to be what we are called to be, like a gardener ensuring that every plant and tree in the garden has what it needs to thrive: not just good light, some warmth, rich soil, and water, but also the right relationship with other plants, through roots and flowers and pollinating insects. "In creating a garden world," writes Norman Wirzba, "God made it clear that human kinship is to be so broad and deep as to include the animals and all the life of the garden. . . . For people to thrive, they need to know they *belong* in their places and communities, grow out of and are benefited by them . . . and can only fully flower if they make mutual flourishing their central concern."

A retreat makes space for God to issue this invitation through what he has wonderfully made, and that includes our thoughts, feelings, insights, and dreams. When we think of creation, we often ignore this "invisible" dimension. Yet the Church's ancient profession of belief, the Nicene Creed, declares that God is maker "of all that is, seen and unseen." Both physical creation and the realm of the spirits (angels both good and fallen) are *created*. Knowing and interpreting the spirits as manifested in thoughts and feelings is the ancient means by which we come to know God and receive his gifts and guidance. It is also the place we discover false or distracting spirits that can block us from receiving those gifts and guidance. In the Church's tradition, the practice of this very deep kind of wisdom is called *discernment of spirits*.

A unique aid for entering into this consciousness of God and discerning his loving call to us are the *Spiritual Exercises* (SE) of Saint Ignatius of Loyola (1491–1556), which hereafter I'll just call "the *Exercises*." For five centuries, using silent prayer and imaginative contemplations, this little retreat manual has helped people encounter and follow Christ more deeply. Now we have a Jesuit pope deeply formed by those same *Exercises*.

In his notes at the start of the *Exercises*, Ignatius takes it for granted—for this was his experience—that the Creator communicates directly with the creature, who opens herself to him, by inflaming her soul "with His love and praise" and disposing her toward the ways in which she might "better serve God in the future" (SE 15). God communicates to us, says Ignatius, through what God has created, both the created visible and the created invisible.

We make a retreat to return to our place in the God-created garden world, to receive good things from our Creator, to hear what he has to tell us, and to receive his guidance to become more deeply *the thing for which we were made*.

We pray, at the start of this retreat, for the grace to desire what God desires for us when he looks at us. We pray for an attitude of grateful receptivity. For it is only by "coming out of ourselves"—the fruit of the Spirit's action in us, to which we open in trust—that we allow God's life to flow in and through us, and out to others, and so become co-creators with him of a new creation.

POINT FOR REFLECTION

In what ways am I already aware that God speaks to me through his creation? What other ways might I be open to?

A Mission on This Earth

It is a sobering thought that most of what we start out with in life has literally nothing to do with our own efforts or choices. Even what we choose and achieve is enabled or limited by the circumstances we started out with. Our parents, our name, our sex, the home we are brought to after being born, the schools we were sent to, our relatives—all these are handed to us, with their gifts and their hurts. I have been dealt a hand, and inside the hand I have been dealt is a little package addressed to me alone, which contains the promise of the thing for which I was made.

"I am a mission on this earth," says Francis. "That is the reason why I am here in this world" (EG 273). With his invitation to know and embrace my mission, God invites me to become what uniquely I am called to be in the service of his new creation.

"The world is always *being made*," says Francis in *Let Us Dream* (LUD 4). But we are not passive spectators. "No: we're protagonists, we're—if I can stretch the word—*co-creators*." Through our imaginations and our desires, our work and our being, we forge a bridge to God's activity of ongoing creation. "Once we realize that we are creatures," Francis said in Budapest in April 2023, "we become creative."

This awareness that we are called to create through service is much more important than other things we might pursue or desire, including success, wealth, power, good looks, and fame. Some of the most fulfilled and contented people have none of these, but they know they belong to God and to others. They have a sense of agency, of being subjects, of being called to serve a good larger than their own self-interest. Just like healthy plants above the soil that reflect a complex mesh of interconnectedness beneath it, these people are rooted in networks of belonging, bound in with others, giving and receiving.

Fleeing from "a personal and committed relationship with God which at the same time commits us to serving others" is a temptation of our times, Francis notes in *Evangelii Gaudium*, "as believers seek to hide or keep apart from others, or quietly flit from one place to another or from one task to another, without creating deep and stable bonds" (EG 91). This rootless superficiality is very different from those moments of uprooting that are necessary for growth; healthy development at times requires moving to richer soil. But uprooting that goes on too long is damaging to us. Among the most wounded people are those who are convinced that they belong nowhere, to no one, and have no role in serving others. Prisons and refugee camps are full of this kind of despair and depression.

The temptation of our times that Francis refers to is a restless fleeing from our roots in ways that keep us closed in on ourselves. It happens when we have tried to seize hold of our lives and make them conform to some idea we have of what they should be, and perhaps what others—parents, friends, employers, advertisers—expect of us. In choosing to act as our own creator, rather than seek from our Creator the mission for which he created us, we become alien to ourselves and to our true needs and desires. We need religion—from the Latin *re-ligare* ("to re-tie")—to help restore us to our primary belonging, the source of our true life and identity.

In Genesis, humans come late in the act of divine creation, in a kind of grand finale. God fashions the first human (*adam*) out of the soil (*adamah*), breathing into Adam's nostrils the breath of life (*ruah*), and so makes a "living being," in the "likeness" of God himself (see Genesis 2:7). He creates them different—male and female—but of the same flesh, and makes their differences fruitful, and he gives them life through what he has made: the fruit-filled garden, teeming with plants and creatures.

What lessons can we draw? We are not independent of the ground out of which we were made but in some way belong to it. (To say "the land belongs to me" is a very different proposition from "I belong to the land.") Our existence is not a private possession but a sharing in the divine life. Our task and purpose is not to escape from this earth but to take care of the earth and all the creatures within it. We depend on the life God continues to breathe into us and into all creatures. Like them, we seek shelter, nutrition, and companionship; and when we live with other living creatures—pets, livestock, flowers, vegetables—we can empathize with their needs of food, water, and protection. Like them, we are called to be fruitful, to create and nurture life in all its forms.

But we humans are different from other creatures in our consciousness of a purpose instilled by our Creator. Even when they do not know God, or reject the very idea of a Creator, humans cannot escape their inner restlessness, that sense of incompleteness and emptiness that is often described as a search for meaning or love. Pre-programmed, as it were, to seek out our Creator, we enter life with in-built navigation aids that tug us out of ourselves to seek belonging. Yet at any time we have the freedom and propensity to recoil back into ourselves, to reject that pull of transcendence, and to set alternative courses. This battle within us, the tension of our freedom and God's loving purpose, is what gives human life its extra dimension. While God's nonhuman creatures reach their full flourishing when they have what they need—light, warmth, space, water, food, shelter, soil, and so on—for human creatures, fulfilling these needs is not the end goal of life but our launchpad into life.

Like other creatures, we are created, and a lot of the ills of our time flow from our forgetting of this truth. But unlike other creatures, we are also invited consciously to choose to join God's creative mission, and so find our true purpose. This special role carries with it a solemn responsibility that is narrated in the book of Genesis. God entrusts Adam and Eve with the garden world God has created, not to plunder or spurn it, but to tend and take care of it as God's partners, and in so doing, find fulfillment.

Ignatius invites us, right at the start of the *Exercises*, to embrace this belonging, to see "that God our Lord is in every creature by his essence, power, and presence" (SE 39). In the created world, says Francis in *Let Us Dream* (78), everything has its place, existing within a larger unity. In God's loving plan and desire, everything and everyone *belong*. This is most fully revealed in the Incarnation, for in the human body "all the fullness of God was pleased to dwell" (Colossians 1:19).

God so identifies with the human condition that he takes flesh in us, cares for us, even suffers and dies to free us from the imprisonment and exile of sin. God is not afraid of our frailty and weakness; he is not repelled by our failure; he rejoices in what he has made and seeks constantly to mend it, repair it, restore it. Nothing we have done, are doing, or ever will do can cause God to disown us. He is constantly available to us. As Francis announced almost as soon as he was elected, God never tires of forgiving us. It is we who tire of asking to be forgiven.

This understanding of who and how God is, is itself a gift. It cannot be willed or fabricated or earned. It is not a philosophy or idea or concept. It cannot be imposed by force and law or absorbed in a lecture. To skeptics it sounds absurd. It can only be *experienced* in the form of an *encounter* with God's infinite love. Like all encounters, it is *testified*—proclaimed, shared, lived out, reflected upon—and the experience *handed on* to others. This handing on, which is the meaning of the word *tradition*, is what the Church calls *faith*, which is not an assent to a set of propositions but begins in a joyous realization: *We belong to God.* In discovering that belonging, we find our mission, our call—that path that is uniquely ours.

"Each of us knows the place of his or her interior resurrection, that beginning and foundation, the place where things changed," said Francis in his Easter Vigil in 2023. "Return to that first encounter. . . . Remember the emotions and sensations; see the colors and savor the taste of it. For it is when you forgot that first love, when you failed to remember that first encounter, that the dust began to settle on your heart."

POINT FOR REFLECTION

Can I remember my "first encounter" with God, either directly or through another? Did it reveal to me my mission?

Principle and Foundation

At the start of the *Spiritual Exercises*, Ignatius declares that "man is created to praise, reverence, and serve God our Lord, and by this means to save his soul" (SE 23). This is the famous "Principle and Foundation from which everything begins anew," as Francis put it in an October 2023 homily.

It is startling in our age to see such a bold statement of what the ancient Greeks called the *telos*, the end for which we are made: for praise and service of God. In Christian societies or subcultures, this was long taken for granted. Faith was passed down through family, law, and culture via sacraments and schools. But the fraying and breakdown of those transmission mechanisms mean nowadays that every believer or searcher must choose, at some point, whether they "hold this truth to be self-evident." Yet even to ask the question is to make a countercultural move, because our age has long abandoned the idea of a natural *telos* in creation. Since at least the eighteenth century it has been assumed that human beings assign meaning and purpose for themselves. We are thought of as self-determining beings with rights rather than aims, who must work out for ourselves what we want and seek.

But as a map for navigating life, this point of view is severely wanting. We never obtain the autonomy to decide our own *telos*, and few of us are in a position to make the attempt. We focus instead on immediate goals and needs, and all too easily end up serving and praising gods not our own: ends and interests defined by corporations and power brokers who do not know us and care nothing for us. Trapped in a confusion of pressures and desires, we feel powerless, forced to run faster and faster, always anxious that we are not good enough or will fail. The result is that we are living through an epidemic of anxiety, distress, and anguish.

Ignatius, compiling the *Exercises* at the end of the Middle Ages, gives us in the Principle and Foundation a three-point map that sets a different course, one that starts from the purpose for which we are created, and invites us there to find fulfilment and freedom.

First point on the map: We are called to adore God, in praise and service, not for his sake but for ours, that is, in order that we open ourselves to God's gifts. In a retreat he gave to the Jesuits in Argentina in the 1980s, Bergoglio described how God "remembers me, loves me, cares for me. . . . And in my praising and revering him, I affirm with my whole being, my mind, my word, my body, my modesty, that there is only one Lord who is worthy of all praise." This truth, he said, will "make us free, with a freedom of the heart that is wholly unprecedented for our merely human possibilities." For to praise is "to live in blessing and gratitude," Francis said on the Feast of the Assumption in 2023. It is "to see that God is near you, see that he has created you, see the things he has given you."

Second point on the map: As belonging beings who are God's co-creators, we are called to make use of his gifts as God intends those gifts to be used. Namely, these gifts help us develop as persons who serve, who care for God's creation, who go out of ourselves—in love—as God goes out of himself toward us. The gifts we are given—who we are, our experience, the means at our disposal, our education, our unique personality—are given to help us resonate with other creatures, to encounter them in respectful receptivity, to touch and be touched by them, to receive them as gifts and to offer them the gift of ourselves. In these ways, through life, we grow toward God, who is the true center of our lives. As Francis says in *Evangelii Gaudium*, "We become fully human when we become more than human, when we let God bring us beyond ourselves in order to attain the fullest truth of our being" (EG 8).

Third point on the map: What stops this going out of ourselves is when we make these gifts rather than the giver the center of our lives. When we cling possessively to these gifts and seek to use them to master the world around us, we do so out of fear, anxiety, or greed. This is the mystery of sin we will consider tomorrow. But the point now is to understand the effect of our doing this, which is to close us in on ourselves and alter our relationship to the world. Instead of receiving and giving all as gift, we become rigid, grasping, mistrustful, and alienated from our true selves. In this state we hinder not just our own growth but the growth of our fellow creatures and of the world. Rather than God's co-creators, we become rapacious users, even destroyers. This is the spiritual malaise behind the ecological catastrophe of our time, and the mistreatment of people.

That is why Ignatius in his Principle and Foundation invites us to be "indifferent" to all created things and people, meaning to have an inner freedom in their regard. He wants us to receive them as gifts for ourselves and for others rather than cling to them or pursue them obsessively. Take, for example, health, money, and professional success. If we have any of these, or all three, we can count ourselves fortunate; they help us to flourish. But we have no *right* to health rather than sickness, or to wealth rather than poverty. Nor have we any right to the esteem of others, or a long life. As Bergoglio put it to the Jesuits, these are "contingencies that do not depend on me, but on my acceptance of them." Sometimes in life we may have them; oftentimes we do not. We can be grateful to have them, but if we try to build our lives around their pursuit, we risk becoming neurotically self-obsessed or anxious. For these things are not our *telos*, the true source of our identity and self-worth, and the attempt to make them so sends us down dead-end streets.

We often learn this the hard way, when we *lose* good health or success or financial well-being. In failing to grasp what we sought, we gain what we need. The place of our pain becomes the source of new life and happiness, opening us up in a new way to God, to creation, and to our fellow creatures. At this point it dawns on us that the pursuit of those goals had turned us away from God and creation, blinded us to what was truly of value, and made us miserable. So, misfortune—the loss of something vital that we thought we needed—can help us realize what matters. It can release us from idols and turn us back toward true life. As Jesus put it shockingly in Matthew 18:8, it is better be crippled or maimed than to be thrown whole-bodied into eternal fire.

During the coronavirus lockdown, Francis said he prayed often "for those who sought all means to save the lives of others while giving their own." Many nurses, doctors, and caregivers as well as teachers, pastors, and neighbors took risks to save others throughout the pandemic. They were not seeking an early death, yet in carrying out their duties, many did die. Whether consciously or instinctively, whether or not they were religious, they made a choice, and their choice testified to the conviction the Principle and Foundation calls us to live by: "that it is better to live a shorter life serving others than a long one resisting that call," as Francis puts it in *Let Us Dream*. Such "next-door saints," he says, "remind us that our lives are a gift and we grow by giving ourselves: not preserving ourselves but losing ourselves in service" (LUD 3).

In the Principle and Foundation, Cardinal Bergoglio told the Spanish bishops in 2006, Ignatius presents us with the image of the "ever greater Christ" who "takes us out of ourselves and raises us to praise, devotion, and the desire to follow him more closely and to serve him." In this understanding, Bergoglio was influenced by his one-time spiritual director, the Argentine Jesuit Fr. Miguel Angel Fiorito. According to Fiorito, Ignatius understood by "God our Lord" (Dios Nuestro Señor) both the Eternal Word of God (the Creator) and the image of the invisible God made flesh in Jesus Christ, who is the expression of what St. Paul called the "new creation." So those who contemplate the Principle and Foundation, writes Fiorito, "will inevitably feel, from the first moment of the *Exercises*, under the sphere of influence of a power that is not impersonal but coming from the person of Christ himself." Ignatius gives us his Principle and Foundation at the start of the *Exercises* because he wants us to be free to feel Christ's pull.

It is good to ask, at the start of this retreat, for this grace of Ignatian "indifference," the grace to belong first to God, the grace to embrace our Principle and Foundation. In accepting the *relative* importance of those things we believe we want or need, we trust that God is with us, and for us, and will ensure we have what we need to thrive. And so, trusting him, we can pray for the desire to follow Christ more closely and to serve him.

Ignatius suggests we prepare for each session of prayer by asking God our Lord "for grace that all my intentions, actions and operations may be directed purely to the praise and service of His Divine Majesty" (SE 46). (If the word *operations* sounds strange, we can replace it with *projects* or *works*.) To begin this way is to bring the Principle and Foundation into each prayer, reminding ourselves that there is an order to creation that sin disorders. Every time we begin our prayer like this, we reaffirm the created order, the reason for which we exist, "the end for which God made us."

God Beholds Me

The danger at the start of a retreat is that, alternating between feeling tired and excited, we gird ourselves to be worthy of what we are about to do. Performance anxiety creeps in. Some of us are like the apostle Peter, ready to run a marathon; others, like the apostle Thomas, are guarded and unconfident. Some are overwhelmed with fatigue and, like the apostles in the Garden of Gethsemane, just want to sleep. However you find yourself, don't believe that this depends on you. It doesn't. And that's why the word *first* in the title of this retreat matters. We can only know and love God and discover God's will for us, because God has *first* loved and chosen us. And right now God is waiting for us. He is ahead of us and he is looking out for us. The invitation to us now is to trust in that love, to "hand over."

Francis has often said—and he dedicated the whole Jubilee Year of 2016 to showing it—that *God is mercy*. Mercy is God's very name, his identity card. What God's mercy means is that God is always ready to take the initiative and enter into our chaos, if we allow him to. "We talk of going to seek God," Francis said on the eve of his first Pentecost as pope, "but when we go, he is waiting for us, he is there first! . . . He is waiting to welcome us, to offer us his love. And this fills your heart with such wonder that you can hardly believe it."

Let us be amazed at this: We already belong to God because God has bound himself to us and longs for us, like a loving father scanning the horizon for his returning child. We *already* belong, and nothing we have ever done or will do can change that. What we do or don't do can neither earn that belonging nor cause it to be taken from us. As St. Augustine understood, we are not loved by God because we are good, but rather become good—capable of love—in response to God's love. And from this realization life can unfurl, charged with hope and meaning.

So, while we belong to many others—parents, spouses, siblings, friends, colleagues—we belong *first of all* to our Creator, because out of God's love comes the world and all of us in it, and every sparrow, every hair on our head, is counted and known by him. All creation is his gift.

"Only on the basis of God's gift, freely accepted and humbly received, can we cooperate by our own efforts in our progressive transformation," says Francis in *Gaudete et Exsultate* (GE 56). He adds, "*We must first belong to God*, offering ourselves to him who was there first, and entrusting to him our abilities, our efforts, our struggle against evil and our creativity, so that his free gift may grow and develop within us" (emphasis added).

Handing over like this is not easy. We need to give ourselves time and space to adjust to the truth that the real power in this world, and the only truly trustworthy power, is God's creative love. To embrace this truth, Ignatius comes to our aid with a tip on how to counterbalance our self-focus.

> I will stand for the space of an *Our Father*, a step or two before the place where I am to meditate or to contemplate, and with my mind raised on high, consider that God our Lord beholds me, etc. Then I will make an act of reverence or humility (SE 75).

Behold my *Creator* beholding me, his *creature!* In his original Spanish text, Ignatius asks us to consider not *that* God looks at me, but *how* God looks at me. It is the way a good shepherd watches over his sheep; the way the master gardener looks over her garden; the way a mother attends to her child. It is a look charged with a loving desire for us to become what we uniquely are created to be. The response of love is our praise and service.

When this happens, our perspective widens. We discover, as Francis tells us in chapter 2 of *Laudato Si'* "The Gospel of Creation," that "human life is grounded in three fundamental and closely intertwined relationships: with God, with our neighbour, and with the earth itself" (LS 66). We grasp the Principle and Foundation, that we are called to encourage the capacity of creatures—including us—to realize their sacred potential.

Another way to remove us from our self-focus is to remind ourselves of how much we depend on others to mediate God's grace to us. In *Gaudete et Exsultate*, Francis draws our attention to the "holiness present in the patience of God's people" (GE 7). As you begin this retreat, call to mind those who serve you in so many patient ways, those to whom you feel you belong, those who support you and have your back. Quoting St. Teresa Benedicta of the Cross (Edith Stein), Francis writes that "the most decisive turning-points in world history are substantially co-determined by souls whom no history book ever mentions." Could this be true, too, of my own life? That at crucial turning points people have been there who have mediated God's loving care for me, and that only at the end of time will I know what they did and the difference it made to me? Could it also be true that I have done the same for others? That my life has had a similar hidden effect on them? Is this, after all, how God's grace often works, through the channels of our relationships?

In a society dulled by the self-creation myths of modernity, it remains a challenge to show that this service of others is, in reality, part of the same life-force that begets the universe. Yet among the multiplicity of narratives and frameworks of meaning since the dawn of time, none has proved as good or true as this: We are creatures of

God's love, and we exist in a creation that is also an expression of that love. Each of us is a subject who can never be reduced to an object.

Jesus treats everyone he meets as a subject. His respect for the agency of others makes visible and tangible God's love for all creatures, the reason for creation itself. There is such graciousness in the way Jesus treats people. People who have met Francis (and I can vouch for this) always say exactly this of him: He attends to everyone, allowing all whom he meets to feel God's love for them. Francis, like Jesus, takes time, asks us questions, creates space for us. It is how Jesus treats the disciples of John when they run after him and he turns and asks them, "What are you looking for?" (John 1:38).

At the conclusion of World Youth Day in Lisbon in August 2023, Francis ended his homily by telling a vast gathering of 1.5 million young people,

> I would like to look into the eyes of each of you and say: Do not be afraid. I will tell you something else, something very beautiful: it is no longer I, but Jesus himself who is at this moment looking at you. He is looking at us. He knows you, he knows the heart of each one of you, knows the life of each one of you, he knows your joys, your sorrows, your successes, your failures. He knows your heart. He reads your hearts and he says to you, here in Lisbon, in this World Youth Day: *Do not be afraid.* Take heart, do not be afraid.

POINT FOR REFLECTION

When I let God (or Jesus) gaze lovingly on me, what feelings emerge? What response can I make?

SPIRITUAL EXERCISES, DAY 1 (WEEK I)

The Principle and Foundation (SE 23)

- *Review your belonging:* Make brief lists (don't analyze) under two headings: (1) *Where* do I belong? To whom, to what? (2) *How well* do I belong?
- *Prepare for prayer:* Consider "that God our Lord beholds me" (SE 75) and ask for grace "that all my intentions, actions, and operations may be directed purely to the praise and service of His Divine Majesty" (SE 46). Note the word *purely!*
- *Consider:* "The Gospel of Creation" (chapter 2 of *Laudato Si'*) and Psalms (e.g., 17, 23, 34, 42, 63, 131). Allow yourself to feel God's faithful love for you, and the strength of your ties to him.
- *Contemplate:* Jesus at the start of the Gospel of John (1:35–38), after Jesus returns from his trial in the desert. John the Baptist releases you and another disciple to follow behind Jesus, who turns to ask, "What do you want?" You ask him: "Where do you live?" Jesus invites you to *come and see.* Spend the rest of the day with him; see how he belongs to God, to creation, and to creatures. Hear Jesus ask you what it is that you want.

Contemplate-Discern-Propose

- *Contemplate:* Chapter 11 of the book of Tobit, about the homecoming of a young man who left to find a cure for his father's blindness. Tobit, who is accompanied by an angel (God's grace) and a dog, carries a cure for his father that comes from the natural world. Allow yourself to enter into the joy of belonging, and to contemplate the times in your life (past and/or present) in which you felt or still feel this belonging most deeply.
- *Discern:* What inhibits your belonging? What attitudes or temptations (in yourself, in the culture around you) erode your belonging? Consider the three dimensions of belonging: to God, to creation, to one another.
- *Propose:* What might you be called to consider at the start of this retreat? Is there something in particular you wish to hold before God during this time?

✝

In the life of any individual there are many instances that offer us the chance to open up to the transcendent, as happened in the conversion of Ignatius. For him, it all began as he recovered from his wound, but similar experiences can arise in other contexts, e.g., being in lockdown, in prison, going traveling, or facing the unknown.

—Arturo Sosa, SJ

DAY TWO

To Come Out
from Ourselves

On the Transforming Power of God's Mercy

Encounter

When Jorge Mario Bergoglio of Buenos Aires stood up to address his fellow cardinals in Rome on the eve of the conclave of March 2013, his remarks, brief but striking, persuaded many of them that the Holy Spirit had chosen the next pope. The speech, which came close to the end of the two-week meeting, did not deal with specific problems or challenges the cardinals had raised. What Cardinal Bergoglio offered them instead was a diagnosis of the source of those problems: a Church that had closed in on itself.

He described how evangelizing presumed a Church that had the courage and freedom to "go out from itself" (*salir de sí misma*) to the peripheries of pain and longing. A Church that failed to do this, he explained, becomes "self-referential" and sick, paralyzed like the bent-over woman in Luke's Gospel who could no longer see the horizon (Luke 13:10–12). Such a Church comes to believe that it has its own light to live from instead of reflecting the light of Christ. The ills that over time beset church institutions had their cause in this "narcissism," he said, adding that a self-referential Church "tries to keep Jesus inside its walls and does not let him out."

The task of the next pope, he said, was to help the Church *go out from itself* to the existential peripheries, to become "a fruitful mother who lives by means of the sweet and consoling joy of evangelizing."

When the remarks became public after his election, many took "a Church that goes out" to mean one that was missionary and out-going. They weren't wrong, but they missed the more challenging part. Francis's first major document, *Evangelii Gaudium* ("The Joy of the Gospel") made clear that he was talking about a capacity for self-transcendence, contrasting the health of "[going] out from ourselves" toward others in contrast to "the bitter poison of self-immanence" (EG 87).

The difference is drawn from St. Augustine's famous distinction in *The City of God* between "love of self, closed to transcendence" and "love that gives of itself and thereby finds God." By "love of self" St. Augustine did not mean what nowadays we would call "self-esteem," but something more like "self-sufficiency." This seeking of self-sufficiency—the temptation to believe we do not need God, that life is our invention—is the "bitter poison of self-immanence" Francis refers to. St. Augustine captures this tendency in a similar image: *incurvatus in se*, or "turned inward on oneself."

We usually think of sin as something a person *does*—a particular transgression of the moral law, an offense we have committed—rather than sin as a condition or state. We seldom ask *why* it is that, as St. Paul puts it in his letter to the Romans, "I do not do the good I want, but the evil I do not want is what I do. . . . When I want to do what is good, evil lies close at hand" (Romans 7:19, 21). In his First Week meditations Ignatius asks us to first consider this state of sinfulness in general and to understand it precisely in these terms of "self-imma-nence," the iron cage of self-focus. From this self-enclosure or turning away (from God, from creation, from others) follow "countless sins and evils" (SE 58).

Ignatius wants us to see that, in opening our poverty and misery to God's grace and mercy, the far greater power in this interaction is God's. Sin and evil can never close off hope unless we choose to turn away from that power. As Francis put it in January 2016, a "torrent of misery, swollen by sin" is "powerless before the ocean of mercy which floods our world."

We open the door to grace by facing the truth. That is why Cardinal Bergoglio's preconclave address made such an impact. Many of the cardinals present knew he had nailed a truth that had to be faced and saw in his diagnosis and prescription the Spirit's invitation to conversion. At a February 2019 meeting of the heads of the world's bishops' conferences in Rome, whom Francis had summoned to face the challenge of sex abuse by priests and religious and its mishandling by bishops, the pope again asked them to face the truth by having them sit for hours listening to the testimony of victims. He told them: "Self-accusation is the beginning of wisdom and bound to the holy fear of God: learning how to accuse ourselves, as individuals, as institutions, as a society. For we must not fall into the trap of blaming others, which is a step towards the 'alibi' that separates us from reality."

Humbly facing the truth of our sin—the world's, as well as our own—and letting God gaze on us with mercy is how we "come out of ourselves," to live receptively, honestly, out of a logic of gift, rather than remain trapped in an illusion of self-reliance and the mirrors of our own deception.

We can't get rid of sin, either in ourselves or in the world; evil will always remain "close at hand." But its power wanes and is transfigured into good when we trust in the divine power of grace and become conscious of what stops us from trusting God. This is what happens in prayer, although even prayer is the fruit of grace. And opening ourselves to grace begins in our desire. So Ignatius suggests that as we begin each prayer period, we ask for "what I want and desire," which in the First Week are a sense of shame for my sins (SE 48), sorrow and tears (SE 55), and "knowledge of the world" (SE 63), meaning a way of living that is closed to God's grace. (Tomorrow we shall dwell in particular on this last point.)

This is not a transaction. We do not "earn" God's mercy by confessing our sin. If anything, it works the other way around: The initiative, as Francis always reminds us, is God's; his mercy "firsts" us—it's out there before us and beats us to it. (The Church's theological term to describe how God's grace works preemptively, not allowing us to pay the true price of our sinfulness, is *prevenient grace*.) We open ourselves to this grace when we humbly face the truth about ourselves, trust in the power of God's mercy, and allow ourselves to be converted and healed (see Matthew 13:15).

This is the core Christian experience: the joyful, humbling realization that we are *forgiven sinners*. We have been rescued, not by our own power but by God's mercy, which "always operates to save," as Francis put it in a general audience in January 2016. As Jesus showed in his encounter with Simon the Pharisee (see Luke 7:36–49), learning to be forgiven is how we learn to love. God's mercy floods our hearts and changes our horizon. This is what Francis calls the "primary encounter," because from it all else flows.

Francis understands his own life in the light of this encounter. Asked in his first major interview in 2013 to describe himself, he said, "I am a sinner whom the Lord has looked upon." Sinners looked on by the Lord have been rescued (and continue to be rescued) from the prison of their self-focus, their stinginess, their suspicious self-withholding. They have allowed God's gaze of mercy to bring them out of themselves to love God, creation, and people. As the first two steps of the Alcoholics Anonymous program have long understood, this begins with admitting that we do not fix ourselves. Bergoglio told the Jesuits on a retreat that sin "hardens us and, so, leads us to forget the path to ask forgiveness. So instead of the [true] peace of the forgiven person we get the tranquility of the one who is sure they do not need forgiveness."

Because sin blinds us to sin, we need a savior to release us. In the words of Bergoglio's former spiritual director, Fr. Miguel Angel Fiorito, "Only God can reveal to man his sin." Jesus Christ, the incarnation of God's mercy, comes out to find us. For everyone ready to encounter his mercy, it triggers a journey into a new kind of life, a journey we resume every time we turn back, in contrition, to the source of our being.

There are moments when this happens in a dramatic and decisive way. For Iñigo de Loyola, as he was then called, it happened when he spent a year convalescing in physical agony and mental boredom from a leg that was shattered by a cannonball. His conversion set him on a journey unimaginable only months earlier. For Jorge Mario Bergoglio, the dramatic, decisive event happened when, as a teenager, he spontaneously entered a confessional in the family parish church, the Basilica of Flores in Buenos Aires, and came out convinced he would be a priest.

He hadn't planned to go to confession that day of September 21, 1954, and was at the time leading his "normal" life. He was dating a girl, training as a food chemist, and planning to be a doctor. But grace drew him into the church, to the open door where a priest sat waiting, and he went in. It turned out to be a shattering, if beautiful, encounter with the mercy of God. From this moment on, the world, and his own life, looked different. He later wrote that it was like being "thrown from a horse."

Looking back, Francis reads the experience, which was inexpressibly personal and profound, in the light of the moment Jesus called the apostle Matthew. It is a moment captured by the Venerable Bede in three words that were Bergoglio's motto as bishop and are now

Francis's as pope: *Miserando atque eligendo*, meaning "looking at him with the gaze of mercy, he chose him."

Being chosen by mercy is not simple. Because of our sinfulness it does not happen without a struggle. In his 2013 interview with Father Spadaro, Francis referred to the famous Caravaggio painting of Jesus "claiming" the tax collector Matthew who, panicking, grabs his bags of money. "That finger of Jesus, pointing like that at Matthew—that's me, that's how I feel, like Matthew" he said. "He clings to his money as if saying, 'No! Not me! No, this money is mine!' That is what I am: a sinner on whom the Lord's gaze has fallen."

POINT FOR REFLECTION

Has there been a "cannonball" moment in my life that has opened me to the encounter with mercy?

The Fall

Why do we resist? What pulls us into ourselves, into the prison of self-immanence? Why do we become proud, self-righteous, self-sufficient, self-referential? Why, faced with the love of our Creator, do our hearts harden?

What leads us to be lured by the illusion of self-sufficiency and the prospect of an empty, self-centered existence? What makes us don armor to insulate ourselves from hurt, then end up using that armor to hurt others? What leads us to withhold our true selves, and put on masks to project false selves?

In describing Matthew as "clinging to his money," Francis suggests part of the answer: that we fear to lose what we have been persuaded we are entitled to, because we believe we have earned it by our own means and power. We have embraced the lie that we do not depend on God. In turning away from the reality of who we are—that all we have and all we are is God's gift—we enter an illusory mindset that the Bible depicts as the Fall.

Adam and Eve at first trusted that God would provide, and were content to live by the gifts of God's garden world. They did not chafe at the few limitations God imposed for their own good. What plunged them into self-immanence was the Fall, which changed the way they related to the world. There is something of the Fall in the shift described in *Laudato Si'*. Before, "it was a matter of receiving what nature itself allowed, as if from its own hand," Francis says. "Now, by contrast, we are the ones to lay our hands on things, attempting to extract everything possible from them while frequently ignoring or forgetting the reality in front of us" (LS 106).

That quote summarizes an account by one of Francis's favorite thinkers and theologians, Romano Guardini (1885–1968), which describes the fall from openhanded receptivity into closed-fist grasping. In the Genesis account, God gave us a power intended to be used as his partners in caring for creation and all the creatures in it, that they might flourish. All that we have and are able to do, in other words—our creativity, our ability, our capacity—is given to us for that purpose, not for our own selfish ends. We reject this when we try to improve on God's plan, altering the purpose for which he intended creation, to establish an independent "Kingdom of Man." In the process we do not create anything new but distort what is created. "Man is to be lord of the earth by remaining an image of God," says Guardini, "not by demanding identity with his Maker."

There is a spirit in the garden keen to persuade us otherwise, that demanding identity with our Maker is our entitlement. In the Genesis account, the spirit that entices us into this fatal delusion takes the form of one of the fallen angels who rejected what God had planned for them and who now tempt Adam and Eve to make the same choice. These angels went from being *mediators* of God's gifts to *middlemen* distorting our perception of God. Just as the fallen angels are distorted beings, so they seek to distort us, twisting us into ourselves. This is the image of sin used by St. Augustine, who describes sin as *incurvatus in se*. Dietrich Bonhoeffer uses the same image of "the heart curved in on itself" (*cor curvum in se*). The loss of trust in our Maker is what causes this turning away and into ourselves, to depend on ourselves and our own resources. Life becomes a grim struggle to survive and dominate. As Matthew was doing with his cash, we begin to "lay our hands on things," fearing each other as rivals for those provisions. Rather than serve others, we have others serve us.

We lose trust in our Creator because we are tempted beings, prone to being distracted. Ignatius calls Satan "the enemy of human nature" because human nature is the Principle and Foundation that Satan sets out to subvert. He does this through persuasion. Satan has gone dark, yet appears to us in the guise of an undistorted angel, an angel of light (see 2 Corinthians 11:14). He camouflages himself, keeping his true nature and intentions hidden from sight. In order to close us off from God, from God's creation, and from one another, he adopts a sleight of hand that is effective because it appeals in some distorted way to the good.

The Fall can happen, says Guardini, only by Satan first falsifying the truth about who God is and who we are. God has given human beings power for God's loving purpose, Guardini explains; Satan, who has no power of his own, can only persuade us to arrogate God's power for our *own* purposes, and gradually make them independent of *God's* purposes. He does this by suggesting that serving and obeying

God is a choice. The question the serpent puts to Eve already contains the wrong answer, for it asks her to judge God's word instead of listening to it and obeying it.

There are two lies here. The first is the assumption that there is a basis from which to judge God; somewhere out there is a better god or an improved care package, one that we can devise for ourselves. The second is that the divine command against eating from the tree is not in Eve's interest and good but instead serves God's selfish purpose. From here it follows that God's rules are a form of arbitrary oppression, an unjust restriction placed on human freedom, which God is wielding to hold his creatures down. (When people reject God, they always reject an oppressive *idea* of God.) The second lie bolsters the first. If God does not desire human flourishing and is fearful of humans, it follows that God cannot be God. "To say God knows that man can become like God by doing the act he has forbidden," Guardini writes, "is to imply that God is afraid, that he feels his divinity threatened by man, that his relation to man is that of a mythical divinity."

The value of understanding these lies is that we can see where our own Fall, our own temptation to sin, enters our souls. All sinfulness begins here, in a loss of confidence in God's promise to provide, a suspicion of God, and appropriating God's gifts for our own ends. In the stories we tell ourselves, we doubt God's promises; we believe we can live out of our own resources, create our own life, and need respect no limits. In the illusion of our autonomy from God is the lie that we are not creatures but gods, and we can step out of our creaturehood as autonomous, superior beings. As Bonhoeffer points out in *Creation and Fall*, this "is not merely a moral lapse but the destruction of creation by the creature." From now on, "that world has been robbed of its creatureliness and drops blindly into infinite space, like a meteor that has torn itself away from the core to which it once belonged."

The loss of confidence in God means, too, a loss of confidence in, and respect for, creation and for one another. In denying our own creatureliness and that of other creatures, we end up distorting both. "With this event," says Guardini, "man's fundamental relation to existence is destroyed. Now, as before, he has power and is capable of ruling. But the order in which that sovereignty had meaning . . . is destroyed. Now disorder reigns."

We may no longer feel comfortable with the idea of being tempted by "fallen angels" and bad spirits. But maybe that discomfort is a temptation. Francis surprised and shocked people in the early years of the pontificate by referring frequently to the devil. He made no apology. "The devil also exists in the 21st century, and we need to learn from the Gospel how to battle against him," he said in a morning homily in 2014. Urging us not to be naive about the ways of the devil but rather "aware of the strategies he employs to entrap us," he warned that those who follow the Lord's path will be tempted, because "the spirit of evil does not want us to become holy, it does not want us to bear witness to Christ, it does not want us to be disciples of Christ."

Francis noted three main ways in which the bad spirit seeks to distract us from the path of Christ. At first it is subtle: a little envy or resentment, a grievance in our hearts, a sense of hurt we nurse. As it takes root, it becomes stronger as we feed it and confirm it by spreading it to others until, finally, "it seeks to justify itself." Sometimes we throw it off, resisting it. But then "the devil turns around and goes looking for several companions and returns with this band." This "second tempting," described in Luke 11:25–26, "is the speciality of polite demons," Francis says in *Let Us Dream* (LUD 43). "They ring the bell, they're courteous, they say, 'Excuse me' and 'May I?' but they take over the house just the same. It's the temptation of the devil in the guise of an angel of light that Jesus shows us in these passages."

New Creation

Ignatius invites us to contemplate in Genesis 1–3 three kinds of narcissistic sinfulness that create disorder in the world and in our lives, and how God seeks to rescue us (SE 45–53). The first two involve, in general, pride and a lust for domination. The third involves particular kinds of sin that close us off from God.

The first type of narcissistic sin is pride, which is the sin of the fallen angels, endowed with supple intelligence. Dedicated to sowing confusion and division, the fallen angels frustrate God's plan to call all creation into fraternal communion by dangling before us the prospect of an independent existence, as masters of creation. But no such independent existence exists; there is only one Master of Creation. To opt for Satan's way is in truth to become enslaved by values that imprison and exile us—values that are diametrically opposed to those that Christ proclaims when he comes to restore Creation.

The temptation of pride is to refuse self-transcendence, to imagine that we are the source of our own light, in which we have no need of values outside our own self-interest or even any openness to reality. It is the arrogance of intellectuals infatuated with their own thinking, the rigidity of ideology and fundamentalism, the self-sufficiency of those who possess the truth and regard any questioning of it as an aggression against them.

The second type of narcissistic sin is the lust for power and dominance. Tempted by Satan to become "like God," Adam and Eve's is the sin of ambition, the *libido dominandi*. In his homily at Lampedusa in July 2013, describing God calling out to Adam in the garden, Francis said Adam had "lost his bearings, his place in creation, because he thought he could be powerful, able to control everything, to be God." This desire for mastery, for control, for gain over others, masks fear and anguish: of being left behind, or ignored; of losing out; of not being good enough. Where once they went about feeling secure in their nakedness in a world impregnated with God's presence, after the Fall, Adam and Eve are lost in a general state of insecurity, exposed and vulnerable in their non-belonging.

Their expulsion from the garden—in reality their *self*-expulsion, for God respects their freedom to reject his garden world—means living according to the logic they have chosen. Their curse is to live "in many labors and great penance" (SE 51), divided from nature and from each other. Yet God does not abandon them but discreetly protects them, acting to order and restrain the full implications of the world they have unleashed. Freedom and responsibility remain; we always continue to have a choice. In the same way, God's grace never leaves us. He always opens a path back to the garden, to life according to the Principle and Foundation.

Finally, the third type of sin Ignatius asks us to consider is the "particular sin" of those who reject God's love and values in a definitive way. This is an invitation to call to mind specific evils in our world that we have seen or experienced for ourselves where all moral constraint seems to be absent. The point is to see the Fall as it plays out unimpeded. Ignatius wants us to feel "shame and confusion" (SE 48) at "the gravity and malice of sin against our Creator and Lord" (SE 52) and to "consider that because of sin, and of acting against the Infinite Goodness, one is justly condemned forever" (SE 52). It is not hard to find examples of horrific sinfulness: whenever people, or other creatures, are treated as objects for another's satisfaction, wherever there is isolation and despair, wherever people worship money and fame, wherever the poor are despised, wherever the strong lord it over the weak, wherever wars are waged. "The sins of the powerful are almost always sins of entitlement," says Francis, "committed by people whose lack of shame and brazen arrogance are stunning" (LUD 25).

Behind these evils is a dark view of the world in which only the strong thrive and the weak are condemned to be trodden underfoot. When Adam and Eve's son Cain kills his brother, Abel, out of resentment of a rival (see Genesis 4:1–17), Cain sees God's favor as a private good for which he is competing rather than as a common good that is available to all. This false story is the origin of all violence and all fantasies of domination. The "spirit of Cain" feeds the illusion that only force can resolve differences, and that fraternity is a sentimental illusion.

Because weakness is disdained, the weak are despised. In Cain's contemptuous answer to God asking him where Abel is—"Am I my brother's keeper?"—lies the indifference of the rich world to the destruction of creation (LS 70). It is the shrug of the shoulders ("What has it got to do with me?") given when migrants in search of a new life drown in the sea. The spirit of Cain is the cynicism in response to the cry of the poor and the earth. It is the hardness that "armor-plates the soul," such that, over time, "it can become normal, silently seeping into our lifestyles and value judgements," Francis says in *Let Us Dream*, and adds, "We cannot get used to indifference" (LUD 19).

As he did with Adam and Eve, God acts to shield Cain from the full implications of living according to his own value system. God's "strategy" is always to seek to break the cycle of rivalry and hatred and offer a concrete way out. Francis likes to quote poet Friedrich

Hölderlin: "Where the danger is, there grows the saving power." We just have to open ourselves to that power, to find the door where it is waiting to overflow.

It is this mercy that Ignatius wants us to grasp. Rather than recoil in horror from us, God comes out to find us and plots a new course back from wherever we have gone adrift. What is amazing about God's forgiveness is the way it uses the very site of our Fall to create a new reality that surpasses the old. However total our rejection of God's created order, God always shows us another way of living that renews that order. This way of living is what St. Paul calls the "new creation" (see 2 Corinthians 5:17), and Jesus calls the kingdom of God.

Reflections by the artist Makoto Fujimura on *Kintsugi*, the ancient Japanese art of repairing broken tea ware, help us understand this "remaking" through forgiveness. The Japanese *kin* stands for gold; *tsugi* means both "to reconnect" and "to connect to the next generation." A Kintsugi master takes broken pieces of cups and pots, mends them with lacquer, and then covers the lacquer with gold. The tea ware can now be reused, but what is broken is not simply "fixed" but has been turned into a new work that is more beautiful and unique than the original. In his book *Art and Faith*, Fujimura says Kintsugi captures the promise of the Gospel, which starts from the reality of our brokenness. "The Fall created a schism between humanity and God caused by our desire to become like gods," he writes. "Christ came not to 'fix' us, not just to restore, but to make us a new creation."

Ignatius, too, asks us to consider how God does not ask us to pay the price of what we have done, but gives us repugnance of sin and a desire to live differently. Barely able to contain his amazed gratitude at this, Ignatius asks us to note that though our sin impacts not just us but the whole of creation, we continue to be sustained by creation. He invites us to let out "a cry of wonder accompanied by surging emotion" when we consider how "all creatures . . . have permitted me to live, and have sustained me in life!" (SE 60). Even when we were lost and closed in on ourselves, in prison and in exile, living as if God did not matter, angels and saints continued to intercede for us. "And the heavens, sun, moon, stars, and the elements; the fruits, birds, fishes, and other animals—why have they all been at my service? How is it that the earth did not open to swallow me up . . . ?"

This powerful mystical insight takes on new meaning in the midst of ecological catastrophe. Although we have treated appallingly the very creation on which we depend, the created world has not—at least, not yet—asked us to pay the full price of our contemptuous behavior. Yet in justice, we have failed to care for nature, so why should nature care for us? Why should humanity *not* be wiped out so as to protect creation?

It is a question posed by ever more extreme and violent weather patterns: the raging storms, the rising seas, the spring droughts, the fierce summers, the wildfires and flash floods. Parts of the earth are becoming uninhabitably hot; entire populations are forced to flee droughts and rising seas; fish are full of plastic; and the land is fast losing its fertility. Climate scientists like Professor Hans Schellnhuber, who was at the 2015 launch of Francis's encyclical *Laudato Si'*, warns that if the world warms an additional 2 degrees Celsius (as is now very likely), the tipping points and feedbacks could spell the end of human habitation on earth.

Just as God does not allow humanity to endure the full impact of the logic of sin, so, too, is the earth not destroyed. The flowers still bloom, and there is still food. Creation has an astonishing resilience, a capacity to endure devastation and yet, through the "regenerative ability" Francis mentions in LS 140, bounce back. If we embrace the challenge of ecological conversion, we will learn to live better and more healthily than in our industrial age. But we have to *want* to be saved, to live differently, to embrace God's design for us; and in this conversion, his grace enables us to feel repugnance for a way of life that treats the earth as if it was a limitless commodity.

God's mercy comes out to meet us, asking, "Where are you?" (Genesis 3:9), "What have you done?" (Genesis 4:10). If we confess what we have done and have the courage to change, to convert, to belong again—to cultivate relationships of responsibility and care with creation and with our fellow creatures, human and nonhuman—mercy can do its work, and the fissures of the shattered pieces of our lives and our world will be filled in, mended with lacquer and gold.

> ### POINT FOR REFLECTION
>
> Ignatius invites us to stand before the crucified Jesus and ask, "What have I done for Christ? What am I doing for Christ? What ought I to do for Christ?" (SE 53).

Transfiguration

As we open ever more to God's mercy in prayer and confession, we come to see more and more of our sinfulness; yet that sinfulness has less and less hold on us as we open to God's power, coming out of ourselves to receive his grace.

Like the buds on a tree bathed in a sudden spring sun, we can dare to open outward, blossom, and give fruit. We can reconnect with creation and our fellow creatures. We can hear the cries of the earth, and of the poor. And we can begin to speak of what has happened to us and proclaim our salvation. God's mercy fills us with a confidence and joy that impel us to speak of what we have been through. The experience of forgiveness is the foundation of our mission.

In one of the most striking addresses of his pontificate, Francis described this transition in the life of the apostle Peter, using his story to chart a path of conversion for the Church through the wounds and failures of the sex-abuse crisis. It is a powerful illustration of the "Kintsugi" effect of divine grace, of the way grace creates something new and more beautiful out of the shattering of sin.

Many years after Jesus' death and Resurrection, when Peter was an "elder" and the leader of Christ's Church, it was the Transfiguration of Jesus he witnessed on the holy mountain (Matthew 17:1–8; 2 Peter 1:16–18) that he recalled as proof of the "power and coming of our Lord Jesus Christ." In the Cathedral of Santiago de Chile in January 2018, Francis explained how, by the Sea of Galilee, Peter, too, had been transfigured by the mercy of the risen Christ. Peter was at the time facing the depths of his sin and failure. His weakness had been exposed in his betrayal of Christ in the Passion, and he was devastated.

> Peter, the temperamental, impulsive leader and saviour, self-sufficient and over-confident in himself and in his possibilities, had to acknowledge his weakness and sin. He was a sinner like everyone else, as needy as the others, as frail as anyone else. Peter had failed the one he had promised to protect. It is a crucial moment in Peter's life.

Such are "the times when an apostle is born," Francis notes. The risen Christ asks Peter a simple question, three times, in the presence of the other disciples: "Simon son of John, do you love me more than these?" (John 21:15). Francis explains that Jesus is not interested in reproaching Peter, but on freeing him from the the turning-in on himself that can come with desolation and failure. Jesus wants to free Peter for the mission Jesus is preparing for him.

After they ate, Jesus takes Peter aside and his only words are a question, a question about love: Do you love me? Jesus neither reproaches nor condemns. The only thing that he wants to do is to save Peter. He wants to save him from the danger of remaining closed in on his sin, constantly dwelling with remorse on his frailty; he wants to save him from the danger of renouncing, because of that frailty, all the goodness he had known with Jesus. Jesus wants to save him from self-centeredness and isolation. He wants to save him from the destructive attitude of becoming a victim or of thinking "what does it matter?" which waters down any commitment and ends up in the worst sort of relativism. Jesus wants to set him free from seeing his opponents as enemies and being upset by opposition and criticism. He wants to free him from being downcast and, above all, negative. By his question, Jesus asks Peter to listen to his heart and to learn how to *discern*. Since it was not God's way to defend the truth at the cost of charity, or charity at the cost of truth, or to smooth things away at the cost of both, Peter has to discern. Jesus wants to avoid turning Peter into someone who hurts others by telling the truth, or is kind to others by telling lies, or simply someone paralyzed by his own uncertainty, as can happen to us in these situations.

In professing his love for Jesus, the sinner Peter is given his mission. "What is it that confirms Peter as an apostle?" Francis asks. "One thing only: that he 'received mercy' (1 Timothy 1:12–16). It is not our own power that has done this, but God's."

Knowing that we are wounded, yet healed by mercy, "sets us free," says Francis, "from becoming self-referential and thinking ourselves superior." In this way, the graveyard of our failure becomes the building site of our new life and freedom. We are not simply restored to what we were but transfigured, Kintsugi-style. In Peter's case he is given the grace of discernment that allows him to proclaim the truth, but now with love and humility. Francis notes,

Jesus Christ does not appear to his disciples without his wounds; those very wounds enabled Thomas to profess his faith. We are not asked to ignore or hide our wounds. A Church with wounds can understand the wounds of today's world and make them her own, suffering with them, accompanying them and seeking to heal them. A wounded Church does not make herself the centre of things, does not believe that she is perfect, but puts at the centre the one who can heal those wounds, whose name is Jesus Christ.

Compared to the Peter at the end of the four Gospels, the Peter we meet in the Acts of the Apostles is radically changed. Just as a Kintsugi pot is full of cracks, Peter carries his wounds, but they are transformed. He is full of energy and passion now, and speaks with great boldness. But it is a different *kind* of boldness. Like Jesus on the holy mountain, Peter radiates not his own light but God's. Rather than the reckless, bungling self-confidence he displayed before, the strength he shows now is quieter and deeper. This is confidence not in his own power but in the power God now can work through him. "Jesus asks Peter to discern, and events in Peter's life then begin to come together, like the prophetic gesture of the washing of feet," notes Francis. "Peter, who resisted having his feet washed, now begins to understand that true greatness comes from being lowly and a servant."

This is what it means to be rescued by mercy. With the gold and lacquer of grace, the pieces of our lives can come together and begin to make sense as a whole—as our story, as our faith journey. We grow through forgiveness, which is why Francis is so keen on our regularly confessing our sins. The wounds of our sin and failure are not despised and forgotten but are transfigured, helping us to mature in faith and freedom. The more mercy we are able to receive, the more it humbles us, for we realize more and more that we really do depend on God's grace to live full and loving lives. And as this happens, we become better able to pass on that mercy to others—to become forgiving beings. As Francis puts it in *Misericordia et Misera*, his letter concluding the Jubilee of Mercy, "Our hearts of stone become hearts of flesh (cf. Ezek 36:26) capable of love despite our sinfulness. I come to realize that I am truly a 'new creation' (Gal 6:15): I am loved, therefore I exist; I am forgiven, therefore I am reborn; I have been shown mercy, therefore I have become a vessel of mercy."

Francis ends his Chile address by showing that Peter receiving God's mercy precisely in the place of his wounds is what enables Peter to serve the wounded as Jesus did:

> What a good teacher our Lord is! The prophetic gesture of Jesus points to the prophetic Church that, washed of her sin, is unafraid to go out to serve a wounded humanity. Peter experienced in his flesh the wound of sin, but also of his own limitations and weaknesses. Yet he learned from Jesus that his wounds could be a path of resurrection. To know both Peter disheartened and Peter transfigured is an invitation to pass from being a Church of the unhappy and disheartened to a Church that serves all those people who are unhappy and disheartened in our midst. A Church capable of serving her Lord in those who are hungry, imprisoned, thirsting, homeless, naked and infirm . . . (Mt 25:35). A service that has nothing to do with a welfare mentality or an attitude of paternalism, but rather with the conversion of hearts. The problem is not feeding the poor, or clothing the naked or visiting the sick, but rather recognizing that the poor, the naked, the sick, prisoners and the homeless have the dignity to sit at our table, to feel "at home" among us, to feel part of a family. This is the sign that the kingdom of heaven is in our midst. This is the sign of a Church wounded by sin, shown mercy by the Lord, and made prophetic by his call.

Francis's confidence in the amazing, transforming power of mercy—in our lives, in society, in history—is as immense as it is countercultural. A world ever more in thrall to technology is prone to the illusion that what matters is what "works" and that what is weak and fails is to be despised. The "throwaway culture" is merciless; all values are relative in relation to the logic of technocracy. Yet here lies the temptation, too, for the Church, and for believers: to trust in the power of law and judgment rather than in the power of God's mercy.

As archbishop of Buenos Aires, Cardinal Bergoglio in 2012 gave a retreat in which he spoke of Jesus' forgiveness of the woman threatened with stoning for adultery (John 8:1–11). The Gospel says nothing of her life after the encounter with Christ, yet, Cardinal Bergoglio said, you can be sure she did not go back to the way she was, for no one who had experienced that much mercy could ever be the same. As Francis said of her in *Misericordia et Misera*: "Once clothed in mercy, even if the inclination to sin remains, it is overcome by the love that makes it possible for her to look ahead and to live her life differently."

POINT FOR REFLECTION

Looking at your own past, do you share Francis's faith in the transforming power of mercy?

SPIRITUAL EXERCISES, DAY 2 (WEEK 1)

Meditation on Sin and Mercy (SE 45–61)

- *Ask for* "what I wish for and desire"—a sense of shame for my sins (SE 48), as well as sorrow and tears (SE 55). I consider the tussle between my self-enclosure and God's mercy in a particular moment in my life, in the light of Genesis 2–4 and the three parables of mercy in Luke 15.
- *What are* the sources and triggers of your "distrustful self-withholding" from God and others? In what parts of your life are you tempted by the "myth of self-sufficiency"?
- *Reading* Francis's apostolic letter *Misericordia et Misera* (2016), consider a state of sinfulness or suffering in the world and the struggle there between self-immanence and God's mercy. Where, how, and through whom do you see mercy acting?

Contemplate-Discern-Propose

- *Contemplate: Evangelii Gaudium* prologue (1–18), chapters 1 ("The Church's Missionary Commitment") and 2 ("Amid the Crisis of Communal Commitment"). Taking the Church as a whole, or any specific apostolic body or project you may be involved with, ask, What keeps the Church from "coming out of itself"?
- *Discern:* How do these dynamics play out in the daily life of the Church? What is my role in these dynamics?
- *Propose:* What commitments can be made to combat self-immanence and enable self-transcendence? Where is God's mercy prompting conversion?

*So what we must be asking ourselves is which are these
criteria of the world. And this is precisely what St.
Ignatius makes us ask in this third exercise. He has us
make three supplications: to the Father, to the Lord and
to the Virgin. May they help us discover these criteria!
Each of us then must set about discovering what is
worldly in our own lives. A simple and general response
will not suffice. In what way am I worldly?
This is the true question.*

—Pope Francis

DAY THREE

The Lord of
the World

*On the Lure of Worldliness and
How Faith Frees Us from It*

Spiritual Worldliness

Pope Francis has drawn special attention to a version of
self-immanence that tempts Christians. He calls it "spiritual worldliness," and has spoken often of the many forms it takes. In *Gaudete et
Exsultate*, he asks us to "reflect and discern before God whether they
may be present in [our] lives" (GE 62).

What is *worldliness*? In the third of his First Week meditations,
Ignatius invites us to ask for "a knowledge of the world, that filled
with horror, I may put away from me all that is worldly and vain" (SE
63). The term "world" here is what John's Gospel means by *kosmos*:
an order that is closed and self-sufficient and therefore frustrates or
resists the order created by God. "When Jesus prays for all of us in the
Last Supper," Francis told reporters on his visit to Sweden in 2016,
"he asks the Father for one thing: not to take us from the world, but
to defend us from the world of worldliness."

Spiritual worldliness is what happens when worldliness takes over
religion, such that the Church makes itself the object of worship even
while outwardly worshipping God. In the preconclave speech in 2013

mentioned at the beginning of Day Two, Cardinal Bergoglio warned the cardinals that spiritual worldliness was what kept the Church from evangelizing. A self-referential, worldly Church "claims to keep Jesus Christ within itself and does not let him out," he said, and, in the end, "without even being aware of it, it believes it has a light of its own." In this way, he added, it gives rise "to that evil so great, which is spiritual worldliness." He then quoted, as he often has, theologian Henri de Lubac's warning that spiritual worldliness invading the Church would be "infinitely more disastrous" than any worldliness of the moral order.

A spiritually worldly Church does not evangelize because it cannot mediate the merciful closeness and concreteness of God. It can only act as a go-between or middleman, acting for its own benefit as an institution rather than for the good of people. It is the Church as a tollhouse rather than a field-hospital, a policeman rather than an open-hearted mother (EG 46–47). It is the Church as a self-righteous citadel of the pure, concerned with its own image. As Francis told a meeting of cardinals in 2015, it is all too easy to fall into "the thinking of the doctors of the law, which would remove the danger by casting out the diseased person" rather than the thinking of God, "who in his mercy embraces and accepts by reinstating him and turning evil into good, condemnation into salvation and exclusion into proclamation."

The choice, Bergoglio told the cardinals in his preconclave speech, is between a worldly Church and a Church that evangelizes. A Church that evangelizes is one that mediates Christ. A worldly Church cannot evangelize because it mediates only itself. When Jesus sends his disciples into the world he prays that they do not "belong to the world" but remain in him, so that the world will realize that it was he who sent them (John 17:14–23). A Church that is humble, poor, and trusting in the Lord is one that enables the encounter with Christ; a Church that is concerned for its own prestige and success, that is concerned with casting out rather than reinstating, communicates only itself. "The first step of a humble Church is to feel itself a sinner," Francis said at morning Mass in December 2015, before asking,

> What do I put my trust in? In power, in friends, in money? In the Lord! This is the inheritance that the Lord promises us: "For I will leave in the midst of you a people humble and lowly. They shall trust the name of the Lord . . ." (Ze 3:12). Humble because they know themselves to be sinners; lowly because their hearts are attached to the riches of God, and if they have them, it is to administer them; trusting in the Lord because they know that only the Lord can ensure what will do them good. And truly those high priests Jesus addressed did not understand these things, and Jesus had to tell them that a prostitute would enter before them into the Kingdom of Heaven.

In a retreat talk called "the seduction of wellbeing" Bergoglio told the Jesuits that worldliness was a temptation above all in times of peace and prosperity, when we run along under full sail, and all seems to be going well for us. It is when we are strong and confident that we become fascinated by our accomplishments, and take God's gifts and strength for our own. Bergoglio recalled the warnings of Deuteronomy: "Do not say to yourself, 'My power and the might of my own hand have gotten me this wealth.' But remember the LORD your God, for it is he who gives you power to get wealth" (Deuteronomy 8:17–18). Despite all that Israel had gone through, said Bergoglio—the trials and the testing, the hunger and the thirst, the many acts of rescue by God—"there is a part of them that remained unconverted, that did not surrender to the great love they had been shown."

The warning in Deuteronomy to Israel is *not to forget* whose power we truly rely on, a forgetting that would lead us to believe in our *own* power, with disastrous consequences (see Deuteronomy 8:19). As Francis puts it in *Gaudete et Exsultate* 34, this is key, for all holiness is always "an encounter between your weakness and God's grace." To fall into worldliness is to forget our weakness, believing in our autonomy and power, and also to forget our dependence on God's power and gift. To be rescued from worldliness, therefore, is to be reminded of our weakness and of God's grace, which is the aim of the remembering of the First Week of the *Exercises*. It is to praise God, as the psalmist does, by meditating on God's wondrous works and proclaiming his awesome deeds, giving thanks for his care and kindness in our lives (Psalm 145). This is "conversion through remembrance," as Francis put it to me in an Easter 2020 interview, quoting Virgil: "Perhaps one day it will be good to remember these things too."

First-week remembering is not selective, sentimental, or nostalgic; it is not remembering the guilt of others in order to proclaim our innocence, or using the past to write a script that suits us. It is to face our sin and shame in the company of Jesus, whose forgiveness frees us to live fully and freely, forgiving others. "The ignominy of the past is part of what and who we are," says Francis in *Let Us Dream* (28–29), where he points to the ancestors of Jesus in the Gospels, many of whom are not known for their goodness or uprightness. "Jesus does not reject his people or his history, but takes them up and teaches us to do likewise: not cancelling the shame of the past but acknowledging it as it is."

In any review of our life, it will be obvious that our many sinful attempts to close ourselves off from our Creator, from creation, and from our fellow creatures did not lead to us being rejected and punished. Instead, God's mercy, usually mediated through others, constantly acted to rescue us from our self-inflicted suffering. Even in our darkest days, when we tasted "the bitterness of tears, sadness, and remorse of conscience" (SE 69), Christ was with us and was acting to break through to us, even if we saw this only later. He never forgot us, despite what we did. And yet, how many people did *we* ignore or mistreat, thinking them of no account? In justice, we deserve, too, to be treated as worthless. But instead of being punished, we were put back on our feet, forgiven, our worth affirmed. Did we do the same with those who hurt us? Or did we, like the unforgiving debtor in Matthew 18:21–35, seek vengeance? Did we demand justice and reparation from those who hurt us?

The grace for which we ask in meditating on worldliness is the knowledge of grace itself. It is to review our lives conscious of what it means to be lost or trapped in self-immanence, and to see how we have been rescued from it, in our lives and in our places of belonging, often through times of suffering and vulnerability. "I shall also thank Him for this, that up to this very moment He has shown Himself so loving and merciful to me" (SE 71).

POINT FOR REFLECTION

What do I put my trust in? In power, in friends, in money? In the Lord?

The Lord of the World

In his speech to the bishops at the sex abuse summit of February 2019, Francis mentioned, as he often has, a dystopian novel by an English Catholic priest and famous Anglican convert, Robert Hugh Benson, published in 1907. After listing some of the statistics of abuse of minors worldwide, Francis said that behind this phenomenon "there is the spirit of evil, which in its pride and in its arrogance considers itself the Lord of the world and thinks that it has triumphed."

The Benson novel is probably the book Francis has most quoted as pope, citing it often as a prophecy for our age. It made a great impact on him as a young man, when he read a 1950s Argentine translation. *The Lord of the World* depicts the triumph of a bland, secular humanism that has banned religion in the name of tolerance, creating "a universal peace that is nothing else than an oppression based on the imposition of a consensus," as Francis put it in a visit to Budapest, Hungary. The novel's imagined future is a culture of great technological achievement, where speed and precision hold sway. In this world, whatever escapes the rational, humanist ideal must be removed; thus the depressed, chronically sick, or disabled are killed off by euthanasia. It is a time, as one of the characters puts it, in which "there was no God but man, no priest but the politician, no prophet but the schoolmaster." Peace and unity prevail, but only by abolishing diversity and creating an anesthetized, submissive populace. As Francis explained on the flight back from Sweden in December 2016, the novel dramatizes what happens when "man's sense of self-sufficiency" passes beyond creating culture "to the point of seeing himself as God."

The action of the novel takes place against the backdrop of the rise to world dictatorship of a remote, ethereal yet magnetic character, the young, gray-haired American Julian Felsenburgh, who is hailed as a secular messiah ("a god because human, and a man because so divine," as one character describes him). Felsenburgh proclaims a Universal Brotherhood, renounces the idea of a transcendent God, and declares that "to forgive a crime is to condone a crime." There is to be a single language and culture. Catholicism is banned; grace is offensive to the notion of human self-sufficiency and natural perfection.

What Benson shows us is a world in which evil has taken on its most subtle guise: opposition to grace in the name of the sufficiency of natural perfection, in which history is constructed exclusively on wealth, power, and knowledge. But the author also invites us to see that, despite appearances, the supernatural is stronger than the natural.

Francis usually raises Benson's novel in reference to what he calls "ideological colonization," that is, a homogenized global culture to which people assimilate by speaking the same language, following the same fashions, and consuming the same news. Using power, ways of thinking prevalent in Western agencies and corporations are imposed on poor countries. In the name of equality, for example, rich countries impose agendas that promote gender as mere social construction, while in the name of economic progress, corporations plunder the resources of indigenous peoples, weakening social bonds to promote individualism. Behind ideological colonization is a use of power that takes no account of the interests of the weak or vulnerable. This power ignores the gifts and wisdom of culture, and does not listen to creation.

Francis talks a lot about worldliness in part to teach us how the Incarnation goes in the opposite direction. The Incarnation is a participation in the power of God, which is a power of service, with and from the people. It is a power that begins in a patient listening and looking, and the sensing of pain and need. In the first chapters of *Laudato Si'* ("What is Happening to Our Common Home"), *Fratelli Tutti* ("Dark Clouds Over A Closed World"), and *Let us Dream* ("A Time to See"), Francis looks according to the eye of God, seeing a world in thrall to the spirit of the world, and badly in need of a savior. It is the gaze of the good shepherd, attentive to pain and longing, and to the way power has been abused and the poor oppressed.

In these chapters Francis also sees grace at work, throwing light on this "worldliness" and awakening people to a different kind of order. The new order is open to the transcendence of a God of mercy who comes not in power but in weakness, not to eradicate diversity but to reconcile it. This is a wisdom and a truth hidden from the self-sufficient and the wordly, from those who think they have it all worked out. But it is readily available to "mere children," that is, to the humble and open-minded (Matthew 11:25).

In receiving this gift of God—God's revelation to us, in creation and in the Incarnation—it helps to set aside, that is, not lean into, what makes us successful in our world: our education, our skills and know-how, our capacity to get things done. And the same is true of our analytical ability, our refined aesthetic sense, and our theological insights. These are good (they are God's gifts!) but in so far as we use them to "win" or "earn" God's love, they can become obstacles, keeping us closed in our categories and certainties.

In entering into this review of our lives, perhaps it would be good to read "The Kingdom" by the Welsh poet R. S. Thomas, and allow his stark words to purge our hearts and minds of all worldliness:

> It's a long way off but inside it
> There are quite different things going on:
> Festivals at which the poor man
> Is king and the consumptive is
> Healed; mirrors in which the blind look
> At themselves and love looks at them
> Back; and industry is for mending
> The bent bones and the minds fractured
> By life. It's a long way off, but to get
> There takes no time and admission
> Is free, if you will purge yourself
> Of desire, and present yourself with
> Your need only and the simple offering
> Of your faith, green as a leaf.

POINT FOR REFLECTION

How hard is it to put aside what makes me successful?

An Examen

In a talk on worldliness in a retreat to Spanish bishops in 2006, Cardinal Bergoglio began by asking them to read verses from the First Letter of St. John (1 John 2:12–17), in which the apostle reminds us of the victory Jesus has wrought. That victory, St. John assures his followers, is also theirs. "It is precisely the memory of the salvation we have received that makes us believers and gives us strength for the struggle against the world," Cardinal Bergoglio says. "This memory brings to the fore a reality: our victory against the world is faith. Therefore we approach the struggle against the world with courage . . . knowing that we can trust to the Lord all our worries, for he will take care of us, even when the devil surrounds us."

It is good to call to mind "the memory of the salvation we have received," to look back over our life of faith to see how much we owe to particular people who have helped us to believe and to belong. The purpose of recalling our faith story is to help us realize how and in what we came to believe: What was it we saw or heard that led us to have faith, and to commit to a life that flows from this? What did we see, and what did we realize? Who or what was it that precipitated that shift in us?

The story of Nathaniel meeting Jesus early in John's Gospel encapsulates in a few verses (John 1:43–51) a journey that for most of us takes years. When Nathaniel's friend Philip comes excitedly to tell him that he has met the Messiah, the one whom Moses and the prophets said was to come, Philip describes him simply as "Jesus son of Joseph from Nazareth." Nathaniel's derisory retort—"Can anything good come out of Nazareth?"—is the response of the world to faith: I mean, *seriously?* Saviors do not come out of sleepy provincial backwaters; if you want to move things along, you go to the center, to the places of wealth and power. What shatters Nathaniel's categories is meeting Jesus and being known and loved by him. He sees for himself that Jesus' power is authentic, and he recognizes it as divine; here, before him, is the true power in the universe. When Nathaniel professes his belief ("Rabbi, you are the Son of God"), Jesus promises him that he will see "greater things."

Once we recognize the presence of this divine power, we learn to see it around us. We begin to discern, to distinguish this power from that of the world.

Often in our journeys of faith this awakening is accompanied or sometimes precipitated by a disillusionment or disbelieving in what had earlier seemed to contain the answer, but turned out to be empty or vain. *Desengaño* is a good word for this. In Spanish, the word *engañar* means to deceive; *desengaño* means to be freed from deception, like Nathaniel, whom Jesus describes as being without deceit. *Desengaño* is to see that "the love of the Father is not in those who love the world; for all that is in the world—the desire of the flesh, the desire of the eyes, the pride in riches—comes not from the Father but from the world" (1 John 2:15–16).

The Ignatian examen (SE 43) is very helpful in being able to look back on our lives in this way, to see the deceits of worldliness and to experience *desengaño*. Most people use the *examen*, with its five steps, as a daily examination of conscience; in prayerfully reviewing the day, we recognize better God's presence in our lives, as well as where we have turned from that presence. But the *examen* can also be used to review other time periods: the past week or the past year or even, in this case, our faith story over a much longer period. The following are five suggested steps for reviewing our life to see where and how faith has freed us from "the world":

First, I thank God for the gifts and good things that have flowed from my life of faith. Who are the people and what are the places and experiences that I can name as the wayposts on my journey of faith? Which moments in particular stand out as moments of "awakening" or crisis that led to a new seeing—my *desengaño*? It is good to write down, at this stage, brief notes—names, places, experiences—that mark this route. Later we will visit them in more depth.

Second, I ask for the grace to see "all that is worldly and vain" (SE 63) that prevented me from this awakening and that held me back. Here I am asking for clarity and insights, especially for those things that continue to exert a hold on me.

Third, I go back to the "map" of my faith journey, and look in particular at my way of thinking and my deeds prior to these waypost moments. I consider how my outlook and insights changed and notice the feelings I have when I remember these transition moments. How did God reach me? Is there a difference in the way I felt when I was "worldly" and the feelings I had when I saw through the eyes of faith?

Fourth, I take all this into prayer. I ask forgiveness for when I was deaf to God's call or obstinate in clinging to the "deceptions of the world," and I offer thanks and praise for the gifts of new sight and understanding. (I may want to write my own version of Psalm 145, in my own words.)

Fifth, I ask God for the grace to see how I might continue on this journey of salvation. I ask especially to see those areas where the "world" has a hold on me, and how I can learn better to live from grace.

To supplement this exercise, it may be helpful to hear from Francis on how the "spirit of the world" impacts the communion and life of the Church and erodes our belonging. Perhaps we can recognize in our past or current attitudes something of what he refers to, which may need amending or at least acknowledging.

One of the signs of the vanity of the spirit of the world in the Church are ideological polarizations and furious battles between "traditionalists" and "progressives." The splits in the church usually mirror the polarizations of wider culture, a sign that the Church has been shaped by the world. "When the Church is viewed in terms of conflict—right versus left, progressive versus traditionalist—she becomes fragmented and polarized, distorting and betraying her true nature," Francis told Vatican leaders in December 2020. Conflict, he said, "always tries to find 'guilty' parties to scorn and stigmatize, and 'righteous' parties to defend," the Pope said, adding, "This loss of the sense of our common belonging helps to create or consolidate certain elitist attitudes and 'cliques' that promote narrow and partial mind-sets that weaken the universality of our mission."

Yet denying differences and tensions in order to present a *bella figura* is equally a form of worldliness. Behind "naïve optimism or irenicism you're sure to find a vain heart," he told the Spanish bishops. "The Church is an institution, but when she makes herself a 'centre,' she becomes merely functional, and slowly but surely turns into a kind of NGO," he told representatives of the Latin-American Church Council CELAM in July 2013. "A functionalist approach has no room for mystery; it aims at efficiency. . . . The Church ends up being run like any other business organization."

In the same vein, Francis often warns against confusing evangelization with a kind of worldliness he calls proselytism. At a homily in Asunción, Paraguay, in 2015 he warned, "How many times do we see evangelization as involving any number of strategies, tactics, maneuvers, techniques, as if we could convert people on the basis of our own arguments. Today the Lord says to us quite clearly: in the mentality of the Gospel, you do not convince people with arguments, strategies, or tactics. You convince them by simply learning how to welcome them."

Evangelization, he told journalists on the flight back from Bangladesh in 2017, is witnessing to the Beatitudes, Matthew 25, and the Good Samaritan, by living them out. He recalled his lunch with young people at World Youth Day in Krakow the year before, at which one of them asked, "What do I have to do to convert and convince my classmate who is an atheist?" Francis said he told him, "The last thing you want to do is to *say* something. You live the Gospel and if he asks you why you do this, you can explain why you do it, and let the Holy Spirit speak to him. This is the strength and the meekness of the Holy Spirit in the conversion. It is not a mental convincing, with apologetics, with reasons; it is the Spirit that makes the call."

For Francis, in other words, evangelization is what witnesses to the impact of the gospel in changed lives manifest in open-hearted hospitality, service of the poor, and a life lived against the horizon of the Beatitudes. Evangelization "programs" can be in tension with, or even contradict, that witness if they resort to persuasion strategies or slick marketing techniques. This is an issue for discernment. One of the warning signs of worldliness is vanity: focusing, for example, on quantifiable "results" rather than on discerned "fruits." In so far as these can tempt us to put our faith in the powers of the "world," they risk suffocating the "meekness of the Spirit in the conversion."

When the Church puts faith first in worldly power, forgetting its dependence on God's power and gift, the Church becomes an obstacle to the proclamation of the gospel. For all its swagger and bluster, its triumphalism and its vanity, worldliness is not confident. It is anxious. It is restless and rootless. It is not of God. It cannot evangelize.

POINT FOR REFLECTION
_____

Where do you see worldly pressures on the Church? Where do they
come from?

To Live by Holiness

In chapter 4 of *Gaudete et Exsultate*, "Signs of Holiness in Today's
World," Francis points to five expressions of love for God and neigh-
bor. They flow not from the world but directly from belonging first
to God. Unlike the "subtle enemies of holiness," which look to forms
of power other than grace, the "signs of holiness" are the fruit of a
life that depends on grace and begins in our own insufficiency. Each
is the result of coming out of ourselves and allowing our weakness to
encounter God's gift.

The first expression of love involves *perseverance, patience, and
meekness.* These reflect an inner strength that is rooted in "a God
who loves and sustains us" (GE 112). That strength, which is the
work of grace, is the source of peace as well as patience and "makes
possible meekness of heart" (GE 116). The strength to be humble and
endure humiliations patiently rather than strike back empowers us to
trust and "persevere in goodness" (GE 121).

The second expression of love is *joy and a sense of humor.* These
are the fruit of the Holy Spirit, which brings hope and a sense of security (GE 125). This is a joy lived out in community, as we rejoice for
and with others (GE 128).

The third expression of love is characterized by *boldness and passion*. These, too, are fruit of the Spirit, which set us free from timidity. Boldness and passion send us out on mission and help us as we meet Jesus in the peripheries, and open our hearts to him (GE 136).

The fourth expression of love is found *in community*. It is when we live a "common life, whether in the family, the parish, the religious community or any other, and so on," (GE 143) caring for others and opening up to them in the everyday "details of love" (GE 145).

The fifth expression of love is known *in constant prayer*. Prayer, in Francis's words, is a "habitual openness to the transcendent, expressed in prayer and adoration" (GE 147). In addition, "trust-filled prayer is a response of a heart open to encountering God face to face" (GE 149).

Learning to resist worldliness and depend on grace is the task of a lifetime. But in the temptations in the desert (Matthew 4:1–11), Jesus gives us the keys. In confronting Satan's bid to persuade him to carry out his mission according to a worldly logic, "Jesus decisively affirms what kind of Messiah he is to be," notes Francis; he rejects at once the basis of all worldliness, reminding Satan that we are "not to take advantage, not to use God, others and things for oneself, not to take advantage of one's own position to obtain privileges." What Jesus affirms, in each of the temptations, is that happiness and freedom are found not in grasping but in sharing; not in taking advantage of others but in loving them; not in the quest for power but in abasing ourselves to serve others.

As we saw in Day Two, Satan has no real power of his own, but seduces us into diverting the power God gives us to his purpose. He does this while persuading us we are acting in pursuit of our own sovereign interests. His capacity to seduce appeals to our vanity. But he also knows our needs, desires, and fears, which he exploits as his opportunity. Jesus knows this, and, unlike Eve, never engages directly with the devil's reasoning, responding only with the word of God. "We need to learn from this," Francis said in the address to the Roman Curia in December 2020. "There can be no dialogue with the devil. Jesus either casts him out or forces him to reveal his name. With the devil, there can be no dialogue."

Jesus' first temptation is to make the created world, rather than the Creator, the ultimate source of value. For us, it is to center on ourselves, to be absorbed in the well-being of material security, as if this alone is the object of life. In his response Jesus does not reject the importance of food and material needs, but he asserts that God, rather than the world, is the source of what we truly need, and what we need is more than the material. There is a human need for self-transcendence that gives meaning and purpose to life. At the same time, Jesus rejects the possibility that the transcendent can be reduced to a tool used for our own autonomous benefit.

The second temptation is the most subtle for anyone with a mission. It is the path of triumphalism: a sensational show of power (to create faith in his messianic mission) or an act of domination (to display God's superiority and sovereignty). Jesus' reply makes clear he trusts in God's ways, which do not operate according to that logic; God is not an instrument of our criteria for success, nor is God interested in displays of his own power. Jesus' life, in contrast, will be lived in obedience to love, which will, in the end, mean the Cross upon which he dies—and complete failure in the eyes of the world.

The way this second temptation most commonly presents itself is in impatience, in the anxiety for tangible results, in the fear of failure, or in the need to impress. These temptations stem from a lack of trust in God, as when the Israelites demanded their thirst be slaked as proof of God's commitment to them (Exodus 17:1–7). Impatience reflects a refusal to work within the concrete limitations of human existence. The "divine power" Satan is asking Jesus to demonstrate is not in fact divine but satanic. It is a power that dazzles and impresses but is sterile, and fades. In claiming to overlook time, Satan's power "leads to the illusion of magic: to control God, to dominate God," as Bergoglio put it to the Jesuits.

While the first two temptations are bids to appeal to Jesus' vanity ("If you are the Son of God . . .") **the third temptation** reveals the devil's true intention: to distract Jesus from the pursuit of the kingdom of God by offering him a partnership in worldly rule. Without me, he seems to warn Jesus, there is only failure; and to avoid failure, you need to use the ways of the "real world," the ways of power, wealth, and status.

Jesus does not fear humility and service; at the Last Supper, after all, he will kiss and wash the feet of his disciples. But he will not bow down before Satan. His service is obedience to God alone, doing whatever pleases the Father. In belonging first to God, he idolizes no one. The kingdom he has come to proclaim is God's alone; it is the gift of the Father to Jesus, who will communicate it in the Father's way, via the Cross, and not in any other way. It is not power but love that will save the world; and when the angels appear at the end, they confirm that this is the true way, God's way.

Throughout Jesus' ministry many people—including often his own disciples—tempt him to adopt a different path, one that avoids humiliation and failure. The temptations appear reasonable, efficient, practical, aimed at securing results in the terms that the disciples understand Jesus' mission. Each time, Jesus rejects them, and does so definitively on Calvary.

Francis stresses often that the Christian life is a struggle. Our decision to live by the Principle and Foundation will attract attempts to deviate us from doing so. We will be "sifted." But, as Francis also reminds us, while the devil with his false promises appears to be the central character of the temptations, in reality it is the Holy Spirit that leads Jesus into the desert to be tempted (Matthew 4:1). The crisis of temptation purifies our belonging to God and brings clarity about his ways, versus the ways of the world. Even if we fall for a time, what enables us to emerge victorious is discernment. We learn what is of God, and what is of the world. In choosing the first, we resist the power *of* the world while opening up space for God's power to work *in* the world.

POINT FOR REFLECTION

What might it mean in my life to resist worldliness and trust in grace?

SPIRITUAL EXERCISES, DAY 3 (WEEK 2)

Meditation on Worldliness in the Light of My Faith Journey (SE 63)

- *Ask for* "a knowledge of the world, that filled with horror, I may put away from me all that is worldly and vain" (SE 63).
- *Read Evangelii Gaudium* on spiritual worldliness (93–97) plus *Gaudete et Exsultate*, chapters 2 and 4.
- *Follow* the five steps above and write your own version of Psalm 145.
- *Colloquy:* "I shall also thank [God] for this, that up to this very moment He has shown Himself so loving and merciful to me" (SE 71).

Contemplate-Discern-Propose

- *Contemplate:* The first chapters of *Laudato Si'*, *Fratelli Tutti*, and/or *Let Us Dream* in the light of Matthew 4:1–11 (the temptations of Christ).
- *Discern:* Where do you see the "spirit of this world" holding sway in today's world, and where do you see grace?
- *Act:* Where in this struggle are you called to be?

In the period of convalescence at home in Loyola, St. Ignatius comes out of his spiritual drowsiness and encounters the Lord, who is capable of filling his life to the full. His worldly experiences as a courtier and soldier now shrink in significance compared to the knightly adventure of meeting our Lord. In this period he alternates between reading and prayer, and there surges in him the desire to do great things for the Lord.

—Fernando Montes, SJ

DAY FOUR

Called, Chosen, Sent

*On Jesus' Call to Work for His Kingdom,
and Doing It His Way*

I Hope in Him

At a May 2023 conference in Rome, Pope Francis shared the stage with the recently elected Italian prime minister, Giorgia Meloni. The conference was to highlight the country's plummeting birthrate, down by a third from just twelve years before. It is a statistic fairly typical of much of the developed world in recent decades, where there has been a sharp rise in numbers of young people who do not want, or believe they are not able to have, children. Francis said at the conference he believed this trend was a sign of an absence of hope, for the birth of children is "the principal way of measuring the hope of a people."

The pope then painted a picture of contemporary anguish as a general fear of the future, and a sense of powerlessness in the face of rapid change. Ours is an age of precarity and instability, a time of pandemics, of torn social fabrics and a worldwide climate emergency, alongside vertiginous developments in technology and growing inequalities, to mention just a few of the major challenges. Unsurprisingly, these developments are leading to widely reported increases in personal stress, depression, and despair—a new "age of anxiety."

Young people in particular, said the pope at the conference, often see tomorrow as a "mountain impossible to climb," not least because high unemployment in a brutal jobs market denies them the stability to plan families and give shape to their lives. So for many people, the pope went on, life had narrowed to focus on the self: to making money, establishing careers, traveling, and the jealous safeguarding of precious free time and leisure. While there was nothing wrong with these as part of "a larger generative project giving life around us and beyond us," focusing on them as purely individual aspirations causes people to "shrivel into selfishness," which engenders an "inner weariness."

This weariness is the sign of a society turned in on itself, he went on. A happy society, like a happy person, is filled with "what generates hope and warms the soul," or that which leads us out from ourselves, to share with others. Conversely, "when we are sad, gray, we become defensive, close ourselves off and perceive everything as a threat." A contented community creates the desire to "give life and to integrate, to welcome," while an unhappy one "is reduced to a sum of individuals who seek to defend what they have at all costs."

Hope is not a vague feeling of optimism, the pope went on to say, but a specific virtue expressed in concrete actions that create a better future. In other words, hope is not something we possess; rather, hope is what we *do*, when we act out of the conviction that it is worthwhile to seek and nurture life. Hope-filled actions place us at the service of others for the common good. Such a hope, Francis observed, "never disappoints."

The hope of the second week of the *Exercises* is not "positive thinking" or "optimism," which are both blind to injustices and complacent. Hope is the result of a transformation in awareness springing from the encounter with Jesus, the Incarnation of God. Being Christian, Benedict XVI memorably observed at the start of his first encyclical, *Deus Caritas Est*, "is not the result of an ethical choice or a lofty idea, but the encounter with an event, a person, which gives life a new horizon and a decisive direction." Francis has often loved to quote this, saying it "[takes] us to the very heart of the Gospel" (EG 7).

The event Benedict refers to is described in John's Gospel: "God so loved the world that he gave his only Son, so that everyone who believes in him . . . may have eternal life" (John 3:16). The first week of the *Exercises* is a grateful remembering by which we grasp that we are created to love and serve God, who stands by us, forgives us, and desires our freedom and fullness even when we turn away. Moving into the second week, we hear the call of the Good King (SE 91–98), and enter into the new creation of the Incarnation (SE 101–117). We begin to contemplate Christ, using our imagination and senses to become part of the Gospel stories, to hear his call, know him as Lord, resonate with the hope he has come to proclaim, and choose to work with him for God's kingdom.

If we have already made that choice, Ignatius is inviting us to deepen and purify our commitment. The mission of hope that Jesus called the reign of God or the kingdom of heaven is a way of being and living where God's law of love prevails, and worldliness is rejected.

Ignatius is realistic about the spiritual combat this involves. He distils the Beatitudes into a willingness to imitate "bearing all wrongs and all abuse and all poverty, both actual and spiritual" if that is what the Lord asks of us (SE 98). Cardinal Bergoglio told the Spanish bishops that this meant, in essence, the decision *to work*: that is, to do what all people must do. For "such is our inclination not to want to rejoice and suffer alongside others that—to stay faithful to the service of the Kingdom—we must make an effort to embrace that which for the ego is humiliation and poverty." To follow Jesus and his kingdom is to follow him in his work and to emulate him in how he works.

It is a choice that disciples must continue to make each day, for while Jesus in the Incarnation and Crucifixion unmasks worldliness and Satan's traps, they remain as temptations. All Christian discipleship is lived out in the tension between the order Jesus proclaimed and performed—"the world as it should be," the Principle and Foundation—and the "world as it is," which is the universe of worldliness that exists in the lingering shadow of the Fall.

Since grace has been poured into our hearts through the forgiveness of our sin, we can no longer live *in* the world as people *of* the world; yet, on the other hand, while we might hate sin and suffering and injustice, we cannot retreat, scandalized, into citadels of the righteous and pure. Jesus calls us on a mission to love the world in all its woundedness and failure, just as he has loved us in our woundedness and failure. And he gives us the grace—and the Church—to enable us to work with him in his mission, with joy. To love the world is patiently to serve it, as Jesus did, and as we are called to do: as *this* disciple, in *this* time and in *this* place, within *this* Church, his body, belonging first to God, and caring for his creation and all its creatures.

As a model and inspiration, we will take the first of Pope Francis's four dreams in *Querida Amazonia*, the "social dream," translated to the place of our belonging we considered on the first day. Just as Francis looks at the lights and shadows of Amazonia, so we look upon our place of belonging as Ignatius imagines God gazing at the earth prior to the Incarnation: not from above and afar, but from the periphery; not with cold detachment, but with a heart attentive to the cry of earth and the cry of the poor.

It might be helpful to prepare a presentation on your belonging place—your home, your land, your community, etc.—to those who do not know it, in the way Francis presents Amazonia to us, in order "to help awaken their affection and concern for that land which is also 'ours', and to invite them to value it and acknowledge it as a sacred mystery" (QA 5).

When Francis as pope visits a place, he greets civil authorities by sketching the unique vocation of that place, pointing to its natural gifts, its history, the challenges it faces, the promises it holds. He often uses a local object or image to communicate these ideas. For example, in Slovakia in September 2021, he used bread and salt; in Cyprus in December 2021, a pearl; in Canada in July 2022, the maple tree; in Mongolia in September 2023, the nomadic tent dwelling known as the *ger*. In the same way, you might choose an object, image, or word that symbolizes your "belonging place" and keep it in mind during today's exercise.

POINT FOR REFLECTION

What is the source of my hope?

His Way

The grace we ask for in the second week is "an intimate knowledge of our Lord, who has become man for me, that I may love Him more and follow Him more closely" (SE 104). This is a precious time to know Jesus intimately, not as a servant but, despite our unworthiness, as friend, partner, collaborator. He has chosen us to make known all he has learned from the Father (John 15:12–17).

Hence the second grace we ask for is not to recoil in distrustful self-withholding but to be "prompt and diligent to accomplish His most holy will" (SE 91). Ignatius imagines Jesus telling us, "It is my will to conquer the whole world and all my enemies" (SE 95). This is, again, the world in the sense of *kosmos*, the logic of worldliness. Jesus calls us to join him in this task by embracing his antiworldly methods and way of being.

To help us hear Christ's call, Ignatius asks us to imagine joining the cause of a heroic leader (SE 91–100), whose campaign or mission is noble and just ("a human king, chosen by God our Lord Himself," he says in SE 92). We might call to mind a civil rights champion, or a political or social leader we admire. Or we might imagine a charismatic, captivating figure who heads a cause we care deeply about: saving nature, ending human slavery or wars, introducing gun control, defending the unborn, creating safe passages for desperate migrants.

Our heroic leader invites us to join a long, tough campaign, at the end of which will be a victory that makes history and changes countless lives. He or she asks us to be available 24/7, to work long hours for lousy pay and little recognition, but to be rewarded at the end of it with the satisfaction of making the world a better place. How would it feel to be asked to join such a cause by such a leader? How might we respond?

Now imagine Christ calling us. If, in the case of the heroic leader, it is the nobility of the cause and the integrity of the leader that captivate us, how much *more* would this be true, asks Ignatius, in the cause of the "eternal King" whose mission is none other than restoring God's order in creation? But there is a difference, and Ignatius wants us to notice it. Both the heroic leader and Jesus ask us to work hard and endure adversity. But while the heroic leader promises that we will share in their success, Jesus asks us to *follow him in his suffering* so that we may also *follow him into his glory* (SE 95).

There is no mention of success or victory. Although we are promised joy and happiness, and ultimate salvation, there is no trade-off in worldly terms. We are choosing to follow a way of self-giving sacrifice, to offer ourselves "entirely" (SE 96) and to make "offerings of greater value and of more importance" (SE 97). We are choosing to do things Christ's way, to make the same choices he makes, and to imitate him in his response to hatred and contempt. In other words, we are choosing to embrace the Cross.

This choice—which is not a time-limited campaign, but a way of life—is the way God has chosen to conquer worldliness and to emancipate his creatures. If the logic of worldliness is the drive to get on and go up—to grasp, to absorb, to gain, to conquer—the logic of the Incarnation and the reign of God announced by Jesus goes in the opposite direction. It is *a going down in order to come close*, a self-abasement that Christian tradition calls humility or spiritual poverty. It is the mindset and heartset of the Beatitudes (Matthew 5:3–12; Luke 6:20–23), which Francis calls the "identity card" of every Christian. "In the Beatitudes, we find a portrait of the Master, which we are called to reflect in our daily lives," Francis writes in chapter 3 of *Gaudete et Exsultate*, which is a beautiful commentary on what it means to choose the way of Jesus.

It's not a trade-off, but the reward is great. We are assured a life worth living, a life in which we are fully alive. The Beatitudes, says Francis, show that "those faithful to God and his word, by their self-giving, gain true happiness" (GE 64).

Showing the kingdom of Heaven and inviting people to enter it was Jesus' mission. He began by proclaiming that the reign of God was already here, present among and in the fields and villages of Galilee, where the humiliated people dwelt. The conditions of a fulfilled and happy life are already present in a simple human existence, if we open our hearts and minds to God. What gets in the way of that opening is clinging to power and wealth and pride.

Hence Jesus' choice of location. In the years of his public ministry, Jesus skirted the places of power, avoiding the palaces and villas in the cities and towns inhabited by Roman overlords, estate owners, and tax collectors, as well as the wealthy neighborhoods of Jerusalem, where the priestly caste lived. Instead, he showed the kingdom present among the ordinary folk, in the towns and villages, farms and fishing ports, where the effects of oppression and precarity were felt most keenly. From there he set out with his followers to the wild borderlands, where Samaritans and gentiles and other outcasts lived, along with the possessed and the dispossessed.

Among these he showed that the reign of God was not a geographical place, or a movement with a central authority, but an event: the coming out of ourselves to receive God's closeness and compassion, the fruits of which can be seen in healings and new life, in liberation from oppression, and in the recovery of human dignity. Jesus spoke of and with God not as a distant deity but as *Abba*, the affectionate name for Father. He spoke of the new order not as a set of laws but as a way of being, born of the realization of who God is and who we are. Jesus came to share his relationship with *Abba* and the Good News that flowed from this belonging. It was good news above all for people who were trapped and in pain, for people who had been beaten up by the abuse of power, for people thrown aside in a society distorted by rivalry.

Recalling the outdoor Mass he celebrated in Buenos Aires for great crowds of people living in precarity, Francis in *Let Us Dream* (122–3) described this dynamic of the poor awakening to their dignity through the coming-close of God:

> In Constitución square, I met a crowd that reminded me of the crowd that followed the Lord: the ordinary people who would stay for hours listening to Jesus until evening fell and they had nothing

to eat and didn't know what to do. The crowd that followed Jesus was not a mass of individuals led by some deft orator, but a people with a history, with a hope, who safeguarded a promise.

The people always hold in their hearts a promise: an invitation that leads them towards what they desire, despite the exclusion they suffer. Jesus' preaching evoked in them ancient promises they carried in their guts, in their blood: an ancestral awareness of God's closeness, and of their own dignity. By bringing to them that closeness in the way he spoke and touched and healed, Jesus showed that awareness was real. He opened for them a path of hope into the future, a path of liberation that was not merely political but something more: a human liberation, that conferred that dignity that only the Lord can give us.

That's why they followed Jesus. He gave them dignity. In that powerful scene of Jesus alone with the woman caught in adultery, after her accusers have gone from the scene, Jesus anoints her with dignity, and tells her: "Go your way, and from now on do not sin again" (Jn 8:11). For Jesus, every person is capable of dignity, and has value. Jesus restores the true worth of each person and of the people as a whole because He can see with God's eyes: "God saw that it was good" (Gn 1:10).

To follow Christ is to make an option for the poor, for the fragile, for the broken. His work is to make known to them their dignity by revealing their value and walking with them, breaking their chains, as Jesus has done for us.

POINT FOR REFLECTION

How do I understand the "kingdom of God"?

God's Gaze

In his exercise contemplating the Annunciation and the Incarnation, Ignatius invites us to "reflect in order to draw profit," a direction he gives from this point on in the *Exercises*. By reflect (*reflectir*) he does not mean, primarily, a cerebral process but what we might nowadays call *resonate*. In allowing God's initiative to resonate in us, giving light and insight, we tune ourselves to God, growing in our "intimate knowledge" of Our Lord and his ways. "The contemplation of these mysteries, as Saint Ignatius of Loyola pointed out, leads us to incarnate them in our choices and attitudes" (GE 20). The spiritual profit (*provecho*) happens when we absorb that understanding and allow ourselves to be changed.

The grace to ask for in contemplating the Christ child is that we love Jesus and follow him more closely (SE 104). We ask, too, for courage to overcome our fears, our reticence, and our distrustful self-withholding. In the Matthew and Luke accounts of the birth of Jesus, the angel asks Joseph and Mary not to be afraid, to trust God's guidance and actions, especially in moments that seem dangerous or impossible. Joseph and Mary learn, as all missionary disciples must learn, what it means to trust in God's promises without knowing or understanding everything.

They learn to do this by discernment, by distinguishing between what emanates from the bad spirit (discouragement, bitterness, pessimism, anxiety, self-pity) and what comes from the Spirit of God (comfort, encouragement, hope, joy, confidence), and choosing decisively to follow movements of the latter (EG 51). In *Let Us Dream*, Francis notes that, when faced with our mission, "it is fine to tremble a little"; this, too, can be a sign of the Spirit. "We feel, at once, both inadequate to the task and called to it. There is a warmth in our hearts that reassures us the Lord is asking us to follow him" (LUD 21).

Ignatius invites us in the Incarnation meditation *to see as God sees, to look as God looks.* What we see is not just a matter of what we choose to look at but also how we look, for there is no such thing as a neutral gaze. A worldly way of seeing is detached and instrumental: we pay attention to people only because of what they can do for us, and we screen out both what does not serve our interests as well as everything we find discomfitting. This is the hermeneutic or "lens" of sacrifice. God's way of seeing is the opposite: it is to open our eyes to the truth of what is happening and to notice what is at the edge of our vision, which is the pain and suffering of our world. It is to look with the eyes of the Good Shepherd. This is the hermeneutic or "lens" of mercy, which is a contemplative looking that waits and listens.

Christ's mission and method are born from this way that God looks at the world (SE 102). Ignatius asks us to look with the same eyes of mercy so we can take part in that mission. As Francis put it in his COVID lockdown interview with me, his call to us is to "go down into the underground, and pass from the hyper-virtual, flesh-less world to the suffering flesh of the poor." If we don't start there, he said, "there will be no conversion."

The infancy narrative in Matthew's Gospel centers on this drama of different ways of seeing: the hermeneutics of sacrifice versus mercy. A child is born; God has come into the world. A few awe-struck foreigners and shepherds rejoice, but almost everyone else on the planet carries on, oblivious. Herod, stuck in the hermeneutic of sacrifice, pays attention only because he senses a security threat.

In Luke's account, Christ is born to a refugee couple who have been displaced by a census ordered by an occupying imperial power. The census is designed to make the poor pay more for the costs of military occupation and the extravagant lifestyles of Rome's proxy rulers, men like Herod. The power that forces Mary and Joseph to travel to meet the requirements of the census is distant, unaccountable, anonymous. An order is given from on high, and the couple is uprooted, part of the mass on the move whom Rome must keep in order. Unnoticed by the world, among this moving crowd of the poor is a pregnant young woman riding on a donkey.

"He was in the world, and the world came into being through him; yet the world did not know him," says John's Gospel. "He came to what was his own, and his own people did not accept him." Yet the few that do are enough for the kingdom to come into the world: "To all who [did accept] him, who believed in his name, he gave power to become children of God" (John 1:10–12). Alongside nonrecognition and rejection (the hermeneutic of sacrifice) by most, there is recognition and hospitality (the hermeneutic of mercy) by a few on the margins. Unseen by the world, the star stops over the little cave of animals, and lights it. The new creation has begun.

Jesus explains in Matthew 25 that the gaze of mercy is the one great criterion that separates the children of God from those who rush on by regardless. On the one hand, I was a stranger and you welcomed me; on the other, I was a stranger and you never made me welcome. At the last judgement those involved are stunned at this charge: "But *when* did we see you a stranger?" they ask, astonished. None of them had seen God; the divinity of the stranger was hidden from all of them. What distinguished them was what they saw in the stranger. The first saw a person of worth and dignity in need of succor, for whom a place needed to be made in their hearts. The second saw someone of no account who did not deserve their attention.

For Francis, the hermeneutic choice (mercy versus sacrifice) is at the heart of the salvation drama of today's world. It is evident above all in the challenge of migration, which he has spent so much of his pontificate highlighting. In the borderlands of our globalizing world, God, disguised as a foreigner, knocks at our door. Whom do we see? The "principal criterion" of our looking "cannot be the preservation of one's own well-being," Francis said in Marseille in September 2023, "but rather the safeguarding of human dignity." The first criterion turns migrants into "a heavy burden to be borne"; but "if we consider them instead as brothers and sisters, they will appear to us above all as gifts."

The uprooting of people who must flee war or escape dehumanizing poverty or seek refuge from the effects of climate change is now so great that if they were a country, migrants and refugees would be the world's fifth largest. Most are given hospitality somewhere in the developing world, while many wealthy countries compete against one another to keep them out. More than two million people have tried to cross the Mediterranean to Europe since 2014; 25,000 have died in the process. In February 2015, two years after Francis's first trip to Lampedusa, another migrant boat carrying a thousand people sank just off the island. The boat was raised and towed to land. When it was inspected, they found layers and layers of bodies, just like nineteenth-century slave ships.

In chapter 2 of *Fratelli Tutti*, "A Stranger on the Road," Francis delivers a powerful meditation on the Good Samaritan. He invites us to an imaginative contemplation of this parable that "eloquently presents the basic decision we need to make in order to build our wounded world" (FT 67). Chapter 3, "Envisaging and Engendering an Open World," explores what it means to open up to the wounded stranger, specifically in relation to migration.

The ones who pass by the wounded man in Jesus' story are religious officials, a point not lost on Francis. "A believer may be untrue to everything that his faith demands of him, and yet think he is close to God and better than others," he writes, adding, "The guarantee of an authentic openness to God, on the other hand, is a way of practicing the faith that helps open our hearts to our brothers and sisters" (FT 74).

That is the true religion that Jesus comes to proclaim, and it begins with seeing as he does.

"I was hungry and you gave me food."

"In those words," Francis said in Mongolia, "the Lord gives us the criterion for recognizing his presence in our world and the condition for entering into the supreme joy of his kingdom at the Last Judgement."

POINT FOR REFLECTION

What stops me from seeing as God does?

The Kingdom

Choosing Jesus and his kingdom brings two particular temptations. The first is to follow Jesus without his kingdom. The second is to pursue his kingdom but without Jesus. Perhaps it is because the Church has so often succumbed to these temptations that young people distrust religious institutions. On the one hand, they see a Church that pays lip service to the kingdom yet does not act to bring it about in concrete actions and choices. On the other, they see actions that remind them of corporate or worldly methods rather than the style of Jesus.

The first temptation limits Christ to the personal and intimate, the ecclesiastical and the spiritual, rather than letting Christ infuse the world and times in which we live. It is the temptation of "self-referential" religion across the rich world that Francis has critiqued with the humorous image of Jesus tied up in the sacristy, asking to be let out.

"A Church that does not celebrate the Eucharist is not a Church," said Francis in a 2023 interview. "But a Church that hides in the sacristy is not a Church either." In the breaking of the bread, he added, "There is a social obligation, the duty to care for others. Prayer and commitment go hand in hand." He said it, too, in *Evangelii Gaudium*: "The Gospel is about the kingdom of God (cf. Lk 4:43); it is about loving God who reigns in our world. To the extent that he reigns within us, the life of society will be a setting for universal fraternity, justice, peace and dignity" (EG 180).

To work alongside Jesus for the kingdom involves choices: about how we use our time and our resources, what we choose to make our priorities. "Just as you cannot understand Christ apart from the kingdom he came to bring, so too your personal mission is inseparable from the building of that kingdom," Francis tells us in *Gaudete et Exsultate*. "Your identification with Christ and his will involves a commitment to build with him that kingdom of love, justice and universal peace. Christ himself wants to experience this with you, in all the efforts and sacrifices that it entails, but also in all the joy and enrichment it brings" (GE 25).

The second temptation, the kingdom without Jesus, is to pursue the ideals of the kingdom but through the ways of the world rather than through God's chosen way. Everything about Jesus' life—the village-girl mother, the refugee parents, the baby born in a stable, his humble existence in the rural peripheries, his ministry to the margins—are signposts that show the way God chooses to save us. In healing and teaching among the ordinary people, Jesus acts not only *for* the people but always *with* the people, through them and from them. This is God's way.

Why does God choose this way to save the world, through the humility and obscurity of Nazareth rather than by the military might of Rome, the knowledge of Athens, or the religious law of Jerusalem?

The answer is suggested in chapter 3 of *Laudato Si'*. It is the misuse of power that has created hell on and for the earth. That misuse arises from the disconnection of power from its source: God's love and mercy. This corruption cannot be remedied except by reconnecting the power to its true source and creating space for the divine power to act. That means going outside the centers of power, to the margins, to demonstrate that power to those capable of recognizing it.

When Ignatius asks us to contemplate the Incarnation (SE 102), he shows us a journey through the universe: from the throne of God to a little house in Nazareth. Just as when Jesus walked in a land of synagogues and goatherds and fishing boats, God enters our world of skyscrapers and smartphones in response to "the cry of the earth and the cry of the poor" (LS 49). God's mercy is always *enculturated*, taking flesh in time and space, in the little and the local, yet opening that time and space out to the universal, to the action of God's grace. Jesus goes to places and people that are peripheral, powerless, and poor. He chooses the path of cooperation, patience, and tolerance, of closeness to finitude and failure, trusting in the Father, as the places where and the means by which God's power of service is performed.

John Navone, SJ, observes that in this respect the mission of Christ is very different from that of ideologues on the right or left, who "promise to make us like gods and to create a paradise of human self-sufficiency where there is no room for gifts from God." His book *Triumph through Failure*, which strongly influenced Bergoglio in the early 1990s, shows how the Christian way cannot be confused with a self-sufficient political program or an elite reform agenda. The way of Christ is radically open to God's gifts and action, and makes channels for these to flow through the world.

Even when political and other kinds of programs advance apparently Christian values or claim to be Christian, they are not Christian unless they are incarnated in God's holy people, and operate within these horizons. The Church is not a political party or a corporation or an NGO, as Francis constantly reminds us. The kingdom of God seeks to heal the wrong at its root, which is the human bid for self-sufficiency. As Bishop Daniel E. Flores of Brownsville, Texas, puts it in *Commonweal*,

> It is the error of an overly aggressive Christianity to propose a program for evangelization that is not rooted in the contemplative gaze, in receptivity to the gift of Christ, in awareness of the manner of his giving. The totality of Christ's active work conveyed to us by the New Testament is a manifestation of how his love came and continues to come to us, in ways that can make sense to us and that invite love in response. *How* Jesus does his work is not less important than the *what* and the *why* of his teaching. If God chose the means of our salvation with a view to our need, the Church must order her practical mission in view of the same end and in analogous ways.

"This is the Gospel: the authority of God drawn near to his children," Francis said at a general audience. Despite being the greatest strength there is, Christ's Kingdom is established not through power or violence; "meekness is its means of propagation." Jesus proclaims in signs and actions that take place in the everyday, in the concrete needs of people, off-radar. The kingdom of God "does not love publicity," says Francis, and "never appears to have an absolute majority."

I first really understood this in 2004, while covering a visit by an ailing Pope John Paul II to the grotto of Lourdes in the southwest of France. Curious to know more about the miraculous healings associated with the famous Marian shrine, I arranged an interview with the doctor in charge, the medical bureau's director.

The "Lady" who appeared to fourteen-year-old Bernadette Soubirous in a series of visions in 1858 made no mention of cures, only that people should come and wash in the spring. But the stories of healings began almost as soon as Bernadette uncovered the source of water to which the Lady had directed her. They have continued to this day in ever greater numbers: since it was created in 1883, more than seven thousand miraculous healings have been reported to the Lourdes medical bureau.

I was astonished by this number and wondered why it wasn't being shouted from the (bureau) rooftops. I learned that the Church has officially recognized and publicized only sixty-four of these cases (the current figure is seventy, or, just 1 percent). There were various reasons, I discovered when I sat down with the bureau's director, not least that the choice to have a healing investigated lies wholly with the *miraculé*, the one who has been healed. Almost no one wishes (understandably) to subject themselves to a formal scientific investigation that takes years, involves teams of doctors, and will lead to a lot of publicity. The shrine doctor told me that each week two or three formerly sick people came to him to report themselves healed, completely and suddenly, in a medically inexplicable way, and were able to point to the moment the healing happened, and the accompanying sensation. Yet beyond reporting it to the bureau, they were content to share their joy only with their family and friends.

And if the bureau *were* able to declare seven thousand healings since 1883, whom would it help? Would it make the gospel more credible? Must the Church shine in order to demonstrate the truth of its claims? Jesus likens the kingdom to a mustard seed that vanishes in the soil or a spoonful of yeast that disappears in the bread mix. He was keen to avoid popularity or fame, and passed through history barely remarked on by the chroniclers of his age. Because if fame and success and strength are confused with the divine, how would we learn that God is truly present in the afflicted, the poor, the sick, and the downtrodden? The kingdom is a *catalyzing* power; it acts from below and from within, spreading tenderness, expanding by sharing and including. It does not dazzle or draw attention to itself. Like most of our lives, and like most things in our lives, what truly matters takes place off radar, in the little and the everyday. This is what Francis calls the "normality" of God's kingdom, and it is why the Christian life is witnessed firstly and predominantly in the daily lives of ordinary people, those whom Francis calls the "saints next door." Just as the anonymous *miraculés* of Lourdes have experienced for themselves the amazing truth of God's love and care for the least of us, but do not appear on the news to speak about it, so the kingdom comes to us quietly, one heart at a time.

Christ himself is the *syntakabasis*: God's coming down and coming close. He comes out to us, in gift, that we might discover our dignity and enable others to do the same. His is the way of patience and humility, of honesty and receptivity, of vulnerability and openness. He works through service, in proximity and anonymity, walking with ordinary people on the edges of places, knowing them and listening to them, responding with his closeness and compassion. This is why so many of Francis's apostolic visits have been to small flocks of Catholics in places like Macedonia, Kazakhstan, or Mongolia. In Morocco in March 2019 he told the local Church (Catholic population: twenty-four thousand) that their mission was not determined by "the number or size of spaces that we occupy, but rather by our capacity to generate change and to awaken wonder and compassion." He added, "We do this by the way we live as disciples of Jesus, in the midst of those with whom we share our daily lives, joys and sorrows, suffering and hopes."

As Bergoglio put it in a retreat to Jesuit superiors: Christ's way, patiently and humbly walking with people, rescues us from "enlightened solutions" that deny agency to the people themselves. The ability to be "inserted" into the people we are called to evangelize is a "decisive test of our faith, our hope and our apostolic charity," inspired by the Incarnation itself. Christ's followers need to be faithful both to the message of Christ's love they proclaim, and at the same time faithful to the people to whom they proclaim it. "To stay in this tension is to build the Kingdom, and the Church," Bergoglio said. "We are universal, but not abstract."

To enter into the way of the kingdom it will help to spend a "day with Jesus" as related by Mark 1:16–45. In this contemplation, walking with Jesus as his disciple and helper through Capernaum and the nearby towns, we observe and assist him as he heals and teaches, silencing demons who are trying to draw attention to him, and unshackling people from whatever power they are in thrall to. We see how he teaches by healing and how his teaching heals. We allow ourselves to be moved by the way he relates to people, making them subjects, never objects. We ponder how it is that—unlike the scribes—he teaches "with authority." We see how he mediates God's kingdom, but gets mistaken for another kind of king. We observe where and to whom he chooses to go, with whom he visits, how he manages the chaos and the crowds and so many different needs and demands.

And then, at the end of the day, before Peter interrupts him to tell him people are looking for him, Jesus gets away to find space for prayer. He asks you to come with him, and on the way you have the chance to ask him about all you have seen.

POINT FOR REFLECTION

How does the way Jesus operates captivate me, or challenge me?

SPIRITUAL EXERCISES, DAY 4 (WEEK 2)

Meditation on the Call of the Good King (SE 91–98) and Contemplation of the Annunciation and Incarnation (SE 101–117)

- *Taking* the first chapter of *Querida Amazonia*, "the social dream," as a model, present the place of my belonging, perhaps using an object or symbol, to people who do not know it, paying attention to its gifts, vocation, and calling, as Francis does when he visits a country.
- *Graces to ask for:* "Not to be deaf to His call, but prompt and diligent to accomplish His most holy will" (SE 91), and "an intimate knowledge of our Lord . . . that I may love Him more and follow Him more closely" (SE 104).
- *Contemplate* the Matthew and Luke nativity and infancy narratives in the light of chapter 3 of *Gaudete et Exsultate.* What does it mean to follow Jesus? Spend a "day with Jesus" (Mark 1:16–45).

Contemplate-Discern-Propose

- *Contemplate:* Chapter 2 of *Fratelli Tutti.*
- *Discern:* What difference does it make to look at the migration question (or any other question) through the eyes of *mercy* rather than of *sacrifice*?
- *Propose:* What is Jesus' invitation to me?

Each day, Ignatius's soul was becoming more pliant, more susceptible to the subtle influence of consolation. "His greatest consolation was to gaze upon the heavens and the stars, which he did often and for long stretches of time, because when doing so he felt within himself a powerful urge to be serving the Lord." . . . Ignatius was contemplating nature in a way he had never imagined he would. Like Francis of Assisi, whom he admired so much, he let himself be open to an invasion of cosmic feelings. But with him these sentiments were transformed into a dynamic force geared toward action.

—Brian Grogan, SJ

DAY FIVE

The Ecology of Mercy

On Ourselves as Creatures
Partnered with Creation

The Cry of the Earth

One of the best-loved stories about Francis of Assisi recounts the time the medieval saint negotiated a peace settlement between the town of Gubbio and a scary wolf. The tale has been retold often, in children's stories and the like, as the wolf being tamed or domesticated by the friar. But when you read the original account, it turns out to be more about the conversion of bipeds than the quadruped.

While he was staying in the wealthy Umbrian town, Saint Francis learned about "a very great wolf, terrible and fierce" outside its walls who "not only devoured animals but also men and women." To everyone's horror, Saint Francis went out to speak to the wolf, who rushed at him "with open mouth." Francis commanded "brother wolf" to do him no harm, at which the creature stopped running, closed its mouth, and came to lie down meekly at the friar's feet.

Francis admonished the wolf but proposed to make peace between it and the town. If the wolf agreed not to injure any more people or their livestock, Francis would make sure it was fed, "for I know full well that whatever evil thou hast done, thou hast done it through hunger." The wolf nodded its consent, then meekly trotted alongside the friar into the town square.

There St. Francis preached fiercely, calling upon the townspeople to repent and change. With the wolf at his side, he warned the people of Gubbio that "far more perilous is the fire of hell . . . than is the fury of a wolf which can only kill the body." If the people met the wolf's need of food, he said, he would bring an end to the attacks. At this, "all the people with one voice" agreed to the new arrangement, and the wolf confirmed its side of the bargain by placing its paw in the friar's hand. The story ends with the wolf living for another two years, going from door to door to be fed, until it died of old age, and was mourned by the townsfolk.

What happens if we read the story through the lens of *Laudato Si'*, and take seriously the wolf as a creature of the natural world? What if it is a parable about people who no longer live as if they belong to creation? The walled-in city of Gubbio, like the cities of our own time, existed with its back turned to the natural world, dependent on it yet treating it with contempt. Nature, disturbed because out of balance, has become an existential threat to us. The extreme weather events brought on by climate change are the result of the way the Western world has massively expanded these past two hundred years, plundering creation as if it is an unlimited resource. "This sister," writes Pope Francis, referring to the "Mother Earth" of Saint Francis's canticle, "now cries out to us because of the harm we have inflicted on her by our irresponsible use and abuse of the goods with which God has endowed her" (LS 2).

This reading is supported by another, less well-known story from the life of Saint Francis that also involves wolves, but with a very different ending. A place called Greccio was tormented by packs of predatory wolves and hailstorms that devasted crops. Saint Francis called the people to repentance, promising that they would be freed from the torments, "and the Lord, looking benevolently upon you, will fill you with worldly goods." But, he warned, if they were not grateful and returned to sin, punishment would be revisited upon them. This is what happened. Absent the wolves and the hail, the town grew rich. They forgot about God who saved them, and "the dung of worldly goods blinded them." Not only did the previous scourges return, but Greccio was destroyed by a fratricidal war and an epidemic.

The lessons are clear. Once we turn our backs on what is gift and come to believe that we are self-entitled masters of creation, the resulting disorder is felt in humanity and in nature. The effects of this "violence present in our hearts" are everywhere now evident in the earth itself, says Francis (LS 2). At the heart of ecological conversion is our capacity to hear "the cry of the earth and of the poor" and to learn again to belong to creation, caring for its creatures.

More than anyone in Christian history, Saint Francis stands for fraternity with creation, which he saw as "a magnificent book in which God speaks to us and grants us a glimpse of his infinite beauty and goodness" (LS 11, 12). Partnership with creation calls for a shift in attitude, and concrete choices about the way we live, as well as the witness we give regarding what we value and stand for. Now, in our own time, these choices are key to our following of Christ. No longer can Christians act as if concern for our impact on the natural world is an issue irrelevant to our faith. At the heart of ecological conversion, and the transition in society and economy it calls for, is the discernment Ignatius sets out for us in his "Meditation on Two Standards" (SE 137–47). There is a struggle, a battle. A choice is demanded of us. Which way of life brings life, and which death—for us as individuals, and for the earth we share? Which do we choose?

The scale of the challenge of ecological conversion we face is vast: we must rethink economics, politics, and culture under the pressure of a ticking clock. As Francis put it starkly in his message *Laudate Deum* in October 2023, "The world in which we live is collapsing and may be nearing the breaking point" (LD 2). The challenge will define this generation.

In previous eras, nature was something we were in awe of and sought to subdue. Later, separated from nature in our cities, we romanticized and idealized nature. More recently, "the environment" was what we sought to conserve and escape to. Now, in this generation, we are called to a *partnership* with creation, overcoming all sense that the natural world is somehow separate from us. In *Laudato Si'*, Francis has placed the Church at the heart of this challenge, showing that at its core is a spiritual conversion from which all else flows. *Laudato Si'* hears the Spirit calling us to a new relationship with the created world. And it begins with facing the truth of what we have done.

"We human beings, in these last two centuries, have grown at the expense of the earth," Francis told the "Economy of Francesco" event in Assisi in September 2022. "The earth is the one that pays the price. We have often plundered in order to increase our own well-being, and not even the well-being of all, but of a small group." In *Evangelii Gaudium* (53) he called attention to the "throwaway culture" of the Western way of living, in which the excluded are outcast and set aside, and the earth burns. "Such an economy kills."

The climate crisis has exposed a vein of Christian hypocrisy. "One cannot claim to love God if one does not also love what God loves," as the theologian Norman Wirzba says. Why do Christians affirm God as Creator and yet, as he puts it, "consent to the destruction of what God creates and daily sustains"? As Francis asks in *Laudate Deum*, "The world sings of an infinite Love: how can we fail to care for it?" (LD 65). Could this be another reason many young people distrust the Church? But the question can be put more broadly. Why, faced with climate change, do so few people embrace the change in lifestyles now called for? Why, despite the commitments made by world leaders in 2015, were more fossil fuels used and more carbon dioxide emitted in 2022 than ever before in human history?

The fact is that we are shaped far more by the values of the culture of consumption than most of us are willing to admit. And that culture has been conditioned by the myth that what generates profit for companies and economic growth automatically serves the common good. "The mentality of maximum gain at minimal cost," says Francis in *Laudate Deum*, "makes impossible any sincere concern for our common home and any real preoccupation about assisting the poor and the needy discarded by our society" (31).

In the movie *The Letter*, Pope Francis tells one of his favorite stories, based on a twelfth-century Jewish midrash about the Tower of Babel. Like certain show-off shiny towers in contemporary New York or Dubai, the Tower of Babel (Genesis 11:1–9) was built to impress and intimidate by its scale, height, and opulence. The tower was made of bricks that were costly to produce. If a slave dropped and broke a brick, all work would come to a halt and he would be severely beaten in front of all the others. But if, during the hottest part of the day, a slave fell to his death, he was simply replaced, and everyone carried on. This was normal, just the way things were.

In our climate crisis, said Francis in the movie, the "tower of human arrogance" being built with bricks of power required people to work like slaves, who, when they fall, are discarded and forgotten. But as with the slaves, "if nature falls, nothing happens." Francis went on to describe the power of the few who "use everything: they use people, they use nature, they use everything and destroy it." This has come to seem so normal to us that we find it hard to imagine another way, he said. But now, in the droughts, floods, and earthquakes, nature is starting to scream, "Stop! Stop!"

> ## POINT FOR REFLECTION
>
> What is my relationship to the created world?

A New Ark

If nature falls, nothing happens.

Knowing is not enough. What governs how we behave and the choices we make is what we *value*, and therefore what we *desire*. What we desire and value (or despise as not having value) is shaped, in large part, by what those around us value or desire. The culture of wealthy Western countries, indeed the whole project of modernity, values above all the sovereign individual who has the financial freedom to construct his or her future and whose success is measured by an increase in options and resources.

A country's Gross Domestic Product (GDP) represents the calculation of value by the prices earned in the market for goods and services; therefore, the GDP is a measurement not of wealth but of consumption. Between 1950 and 2010 the world's population tripled and world GDP increased sevenfold, fossil-fuel energy use quadrupled, and fertilizer use rose more than tenfold. Now the richest 1 percent own more wealth than all the other 99 percent put together; two billion people live on less than three dollars a day; one in eight people are out of work.

Rising global temperatures threaten a scale and intensity of extreme weather events never seen in our history, triggering mass migration from drought-stricken and flooded areas. As a result of industrialized agriculture, the world produces far more food than it needs, and throws much of it away. Around 40 percent of the agricultural land of the world is now seriously degraded. Ultra-processed food, which makes up more than 50 percent of the diet consumed by Brits and Americans, is behind an epidemic of obesity and heart problems. The warning signs are everywhere that we have reached, and breached, the carrying capacity of the planet. Yet GDP growth remains the core aim of Western economic policy.

For what is valued—politically and culturally—is more growth, more profit, more accumulation of goods and freedoms. The value that is ignored by this metric is the value of other kinds of activity or production: people voluntarily caring for one another, the health of the natural world, the distribution of wealth, and the quality of housing and labor. Nor does it measure other social and personal goods: participation, education, a sense of belonging. In *Let Us Dream*, Francis cites economist Mariana Mazzucato's observation that since the late nineteenth century we have gone from "value determining price" to "price determining value." Obsessed with growth, we have forgotten to ask how to thrive—and how the earth can thrive with us.

Gaël Giraud, SJ, the economist who champions Francis's call for an ecological transition, notes how "the life of a human being, or of one of the one hundred million sharks we kill each year, or of a tree, is not capital. Its value is immeasurable. It cannot be identified independently of the relationships that constitute it." The modern, technocratic way of looking at the world, focusing on the individual in isolation from the relationships in which she is embedded, is a rejection of what Giraud calls the "relational cosmology" of Christianity that is expressed in *Laudato Si'*.

The narrow lenses of the technocratic mindset fail to include what has true worth, because they exclude the broader bonds of belonging: Creator-creation-creatures. The human-centered, self-enclosed outlook of the modern era, especially from the seventeenth century, still dominates, as symbolized in Leonardo da Vinci's *Vitruvian Man*: a masculine figure, white, alone, free of all vulnerability or blemish, and armed with the geometry he needs to dominate the world. Nature, disregarded as inert, passive, lacking in soul or spirit, is absent.

Vitruvian Man rests on a misdiagnosis: that we are independent, sovereign individuals, and that other people, and creation itself, are little more than an extrinsic mechanism for meeting our needs. As Giraud notes, for centuries slaves were one of the major sources of capital. But a slave can only be made a source of capital by severing a human being from any relationship with his or her own self, reducing him or her to a mere object, the property of another. Now the same error feeds the illusions of the neoliberal market economy, that the natural world can be endlessly exploited and commodified as if it were an inert object of no value. We have but one planet to live on, and it has reached a breaking point. If all lived as Americans do, we would need five planets.

In the midst of the ecological crisis, Francis is calling us to a conversion in our way of thinking and living. It involves recovering the Principle and Foundation, and rejecting Vitruvian Man. The Principle and Foundation assumes our interconnectedness and mutual dependence; it offers the criterion on which our economy needs to be based if we are to emerge better from this crisis. In chapters 4 and 5 of *Laudato Si*, Francis shows the big shift in thinking that this will require—a transition at least as significant as any of the great historical "changes of era" that humankind has faced. But knowing it needs to happen will not be enough without the spiritual conversion on which ecological conversion depends. "There can be no renewal of our relationship with nature without a renewal of humanity itself," Francis says (LS 118).

This may not be easy. Many of us spend most of our time indoors, scrolling screens, in cities of concrete and glass. We move from office complexes to shopping centers that communicate a world available to purchase. Companion animals like dogs and cats are treated as privileged family members while the meat we eat depends on keeping livestock in degrading industrial conditions, enduring appalling, degrading stress. Severed from the "natural world"—the very term suggests we do not live in it—we find it hard to "see" nature or let it speak to us, even as we feel the sadness and anxiety of its loss. Even when we see nature as a place to escape to and connect with, we put nature at risk of being treated as just another kind of resource, a place to occasionally visit and enjoy rather than be rooted in and entwined with.

We need "new convictions, attitudes and forms of life" (LS 202) if we are to find the "ark" to carry us out from not just floods but also droughts and the soaring temperatures that within decades will make large parts of the globe uninhabitable. As in Noah's ark, these new attitudes and convictions will involve people and creatures traveling together into a different future, one that seeks to respect limits, curb the reckless pursuit of wealth and power, and look out for the poor and those living on the margins. It will be a society of the Sabbath and Jubilee, of patterns of regeneration of relationships and the land, a time "for the poor to find fresh hope, for people to find their souls again," as Francis puts it in Let Us Dream. This is humanity's "Noah moment," he adds, where the extinction we face opens us to another way, governed by an ecology of mercy. "This is the grace available to us now," Francis says. "Let us not throw it away" (LUD 15).

We open ourselves to that grace by making room for God to speak to us through creation, to undergo the "ecological conversion" that the modern popes have been calling us to (St. John Paul II was the first to use the phrase). An ecological conversion is to awaken to the value of creation and to be moved to care for it. Francis himself underwent that conversion late in his life, when he heard from the Brazilian and other bishops at the 2007 Aparecida meeting of the Latin-American Church. He began to hear more and more stories, and "my eyes were opened. It was like an awakening," he says in *Let Us Dream* (31). He discerned that this awareness was of God, for "it was a spiritual experience of the sort Saint Ignatius describes as like drops of water on a sponge: gentle, silent, but insistent." He began to see how "humanity's fate is inseparably bound up with that of our common home" and how "humanity is getting ever sicker along with our common home, with our environment, with creation."

Elected pope six years after Aparecida, Francis would in 2015 write one of the greatest of all social encyclicals, *Laudato Si'*, on the breakdown of humanity's relationship with creation and that path to a new partnership. Four years after *Laudato Si'*, in 2019, Francis called the special synod on Amazonia. At that synod, the testimony of indigenous peoples was key. Francis has frequently drawn attention to the wisdom of peoples whose cultures have retained a deep link with nature, a wisdom that modern Westerners must relearn.

This link of humans to nature is a link taken for granted in the Bible. Jesus spent most of his public ministry outdoors, in and among farming people, withdrawing to pray on hilltops and in caves. When he spoke in agrarian metaphors about the kingdom of God, he was not using the language of a bygone era but communicating who and how God is in the world that people understood well. The lost sheep and mustard seeds and fig trees reflect the kingdom that God promises in Hosea 2:18: "I will make for you a covenant on that day with the wild animals, the birds of the air, and the creeping things of the ground."

In today's exercise, it is good to go outside to resonate with this covenant, to feel the *ruah*—God's life-spirit—in the plants, trees, birds, and insects. There we can contemplate the interdependence and interconnectedness of creation, to sense "the maternal heartbeat of the earth," and to "harmonize our own rhythms of life with those of creation," as Francis put it when he was in Canada.

It is a retuning that starts with pain at the loss of biodiversity. During the writing of this chapter, news came of ten thousand Emperor penguin chicks dying in the sea. The ice floes in Antarctica where the penguins lay their eggs and care for their offspring now melt so fast that they are forced into the sea before developing their feathers. Experts have warned us that the Emperor penguins are likely to die out. It is just one example. Wildlife populations have collapsed by more than two-thirds in my lifetime. Because of reckless human domination, "thousands of species will no longer give glory to God by their very existence, nor convey their message to us," says Francis. "We have no such right" (LS 33).

Yet if this makes us sad and angry, we can also find hope in a lonely hedgerow, a single tree, an uncut patch of lawn. As Gerard Manley Hopkins puts it in his poem "God's Grandeur," "And for all this, nature is never spent; / There lives the dearest freshness deep down things." The Creator Spirit continues to hover over the world, offering to re-create from the forgotten and disregarded edges of things. But this is hope, not complacency. The question remains whether humanity can value creation enough to convert our way of living in time to avoid catastrophe on a level greater than the one we are now living through.

When Jesus looks with love at the restless young man (see Mark 10:21), he shows us, says Francis, "the way to overcome that unhealthy anxiety which makes us superficial, aggressive and compulsive consumers" (LS 226). The vanity and anxiety underpinning our economy—with its myth of scarcity, its ruthless competitiveness—are exposed when, with Jesus, we consider the lilies of the field or the sparrows in the trees. In Christ, we have a God-given model of one who embodies this way of being in and with the world. "The Lord, who is the first to care for us, teaches us to care for our brothers and sisters and the environment which he daily gives us," says Francis in *Querida Amazonia*. "This is the first ecology that we need" (QA 41).

The Two Standards

If the origin of the ecological crisis lies in a narrowing of our focus to self-interest and gain, what can save us? What prevents us from seeing the broader value and interconnectedness of God's creation, and how can we free ourselves to embrace it? A large part of the answer is in the "Meditation on Two Standards" (SE 137–47). In this most famous of his exercises, Ignatius asks us to picture Lucifer (another name for Satan) and Jesus on a battlefield with their respective armies, each holding a flag, or standard. Each leader gives his army a briefing before sending them out into the world to wage spiritual war.

Lucifer, "his appearance inspiring horror and terror" (SE 140), addresses his minions on the smoking plains of Babylon, urging them to "lay snares for men and bind them with chains," tempting them to desire wealth and honor, and so lead them into "overweening pride" (SE 142). His message may be summarized as *Look at all I have and can be.*

Jesus, on the other hand, speaks to his followers "in a lowly place in a great plain about the region of Jerusalem." In that "beautiful and attractive" (SE 144) setting he asks them to take to all people his "sacred doctrine" (SE 145), and entice them to desire spiritual and material poverty instead of wealth, humiliations in place of honor, and humility rather than pride. His message may be summarized as *Look at all God has given me.*

Both Satan and Christ are sending their followers out to emulate *desires*. The great thinker René Girard described the imitation of what someone else wants as "mimetic desire." When we desire to be like another person, we desire what they desire. Desire, then, always involves a model, one who shows us what to want. Here Ignatius shows us two models, each of whom is inviting us to desire what they desire and to organize our lives accordingly.

There is nothing wrong per se with mimetic desire; it is how humans are made, and what allows us to grow and learn. We are attracted to a model, and as the connection deepens, we desire more and more what the model desires. But there are healthy models who allow us to discover and act on our true desires, and there are other models who keep us trapped in what they, not we, want. These are the kinds of desires that are purely "imitated." Consider Don Quixote, brooding alone in his room as he read fanciful novels of the courtly era. He dreamed of being a knight errant like Amadis of Gaul, and became a slave to that illusion, living out his life as a (glorious) caricature of a knight. Ignatius of Loyola, lying in his castle bed with a shattered leg, also dreamed of being like Amadis. Yet after he (reluctantly) picked up a book about the lives of the saints, he discovered that his true desire was to imitate people like Saint Francis of Assisi.

Ignatius, who learned to distinguish the spirits within him, began to see that the knightly daydreams did not last, whereas the dreams of following the examples of the saints produced in him feelings of vitality and peace that did not disappear. The more Ignatius searched to know, and desired to follow, God's will, the more he became who he was uniquely called to be. The saints were helpful models in his journey; eventually, he outgrew them, but they led him to Christ, the true model. His life became immensely fruitful and creative in the service of Christ's kingdom, but he served in his unique way. He ended up a saint too, but a very different one.

Crises in our lives often lead to freeing ourselves from unhealthy desires we have been imitating. Giovanni Bernardone was one kind of model before his conversion, and another one after. As a wealthy young man in Assisi, he was (in the words of his biographer, Brother Thomas) "frivolous and conceited," "haughty and lavish." He was courted and admired; people wanted to be like him—or the image he projected. But through a crisis he discovered his true desires. In 1206, at the age of twenty-six, he stripped himself of those lavish clothes and renounced all his property. Francis of Assisi evolved into another kind of model whom hundreds of thousands have since imitated by taking vows of poverty, wearing an unadorned brown robe, caring for the poor and for nature, and living lives of compelling, fruitful creativity.

In *Gaudete et Exsultate* Francis extends an invitation to discern "the call to holiness that the Lord addresses to each of us" (GE 10). While we may take inspiration from many examples of holiness, it is important "that each believer discern his or her own path . . . rather than hopelessly trying to imitate something not meant for them" (GE 11). "To be holy does not require being . . . a priest or a religious" or withdrawing from the world to spend time in prayer (GE 14). "Holiness, in the end, is the fruit of the Holy Spirit in your life" (GE 15). What matters is to embrace our "mission in Christ" and unite with him by contemplating the mysteries of his earthly life—his hidden life, his closeness to the outcast, his poverty, and other ways he demonstrated self-sacrificing love. "The contemplation of these mysteries, as St. Ignatius of Loyola pointed out, leads us to incarnate them in our choices and attitudes" (GE 20).

The same has to happen if we are to be ecologically converted. Satan's was the first example of the marketing method known by its acronym AIDA: making you Aware, provoking your Interest, turning your interest into Desire, and moving you to Act on that desire by buying. Eve paid no attention to the fruit in the middle of the garden until Satan's desire for it persuaded her that she had to have it. She and Adam had no wish to be masters of the universe until Satan instilled the ambition—which was, of course, *his* desire—in them.

When we find ourselves caught in what Francis in *Laudato Si'* calls "a whirlwind of needless buying and spending" (LS 203), are we acting out of our true desires or are we imitating other people? Unconscious desire imitation—AIDA—is at the heart of contemporary consumerism, and consumerism is a major factor driving climate change. Each of us must look at how much our lifestyles reflect the desires of the models of culture and the marketplace. Discerning our true desires is key not just to our own health and spiritual well-being but to the health and well-being of the earth.

The grace we ask for in the prelude to the Meditation is "a knowledge of the deceits of the rebel chief and help to guard myself against them." We also ask "for a knowledge of the true life exemplified in the sovereign and true Commander, and the grace to imitate Him" (139). One model relies on deceiving our true desires; the other offers us the true life we desire deep down.

What Lucifer models is the *desire for appropriation*. We naturally and instinctively desire freedom and self-fulfillment; through AIDA we are persuaded by certain models that we can attain these things through acquisition. A solitary car being driven fast by a handsome, rugged driver through a beautiful landscape may trigger a desire for the car because we desire to have what the driver appears to have. The yearning for the car is purely an imitated desire.

On social media, which has blended with the market, clever algorithms feed our desires for appropriation, increasing our self-focus and surrounding us with models. We are encouraged to focus on self-enhancement (status and personal success) rather than on self-transcendence (concern for the well-being of others and the common good). And because status and success can be measured only in comparison with others, we enter a state of anxiety in which others become rivals. As Francis says, "Obsession with a consumerist lifestyle, above all when few people are capable of maintaining it, can only lead to violence and mutual destruction" (LS 204). It also leads to the destruction of the planet.

But something else happens too. In focusing on our own wealth and status, we become blind to the bigger picture of what life is for. Farmers who focus on increasing yields at any cost stop seeing the other goods of agriculture: feeding the community, caring for the land, enabling diversity of species. Bankers obsessed with their bonuses cease to see how investment can raise living standards. Academics preoccupied with recognition and honors no longer regard their career as a service to the formation of young minds. In each case, narrowing desire to acquisition of "riches, honor, pride" closes us in on ourselves, blinding us to what is truly of value. We no longer work for the common good but for our own benefit.

Christ's invitation is to renounce the desire for acquisition in the first place, to focus on our true needs rather than on satisfying imitated desires. This is poverty of spirit: to realize that our true desires are met in God's gifts, and therefore nothing can possess us. This is what Christ models. The second grace we ask for, the desire to imitate Christ (SE 139), is to ask to be be freed from the hall of mirrors of frenetic consumption by making Christ's choices and attitudes our own. Ignatius asks us not just to accept humiliation but to *want* it, because only when my heart is free of ambition for myself am I immune to unconscious imitative desire.

Only then can we begin to think about what is in the interests of our fellow nonhuman creatures. Only then can we hear the cry of the earth. To live a materially humble or simple life is to be restored to the *humus*, to the earth; it is to belong again to Creator, creation, and creatures. Desiring poverty of spirit and humiliation, I want to belong first to God, who created me and loves me and who I trust will look after me. But I also want to belong to creation, which sustains me. If worldly success comes my way, I can use it for God's kingdom, and God's earth. I desire not self-enhancement but self-transcendence: to live out of concern for the common good, and to serve the well-being of other creatures. In this way of living and desiring, I am free to do what God does and that to which Jesus is dedicated, namely, the care of creation and creatures. I can share in God's life of love. I can use my freedom—my creativity, my choices—to seek out and purchase alternatives to what harms me and harms creation. Remember the "hidden power" of God's action in the world. As Francis explains in *Laudate Deum*, efforts to reduce waste and pollution and consume with prudence create a new culture, bringing about "large processes of transformation rising from deep within society" (LD 71).

Since God's love cannot be earned or appropriated (because it is freely given to all, without conditions), in desiring to live this way, I do not enter into competition with others. In belonging first to God and to creation, I stop no one else from doing the same; when they do, I can rejoice that we are brothers and sisters, bound by a shared love for "a Father who creates and who alone owns the world" (LS 75).

In Gaël Giraud's words, Christianity is "the religion of the love of God as a common good." Religion that has sought to privatize that common good, appropriating God for personal gain (such as status), acts as an obstacle to all people belonging to God, and is corrupt. Ecological conversion in *Laudato Si'* means awakening to a way of thinking and operating organized on that same principle: just as God's love is a common good, so is his creation. The goods of the earth, and the earth itself, should be available to all. We can desire a life of sobriety for the sake of a healthy planet. We can renounce individualism for the sake of the *cummunus* (from which we get the words *community* and *common*). Freed from rivalry, we can live together as partners in our common home.

> ## POINT FOR REFLECTION
>
> Does the way I live reflect my true desires and values?

A Time to Choose

In September 2023, during a moment of reflection in the southern French port city of Marseille, Francis stood with other religious leaders nearby a monument dedicated to migrants lost at sea. He quoted from the final pages of a little book he had often over the previous year urged people to read. The book, written by a Guinean migrant named Ibrahima Balde, is an account of his odyssey to Europe. The pope quoted Balde's description of a moment when his fragile inflatable, its compass having malfunctioned, was lost in the Mediterranean Sea. "When you're sitting like that on the sea," Balde wrote, "you find yourself in the middle of a crossing: one way is life, one way is death. At sea, there's no other way out."

Francis told the leaders that humanity, too, faced a crossroads: "On the one hand, there is fraternity, which makes the human community flourish with goodness; on the other there is indifference, which bloodies the Mediterranean."

The "Meditation on the Two Standards" brings us to our own crossroads: What world do we desire? Do we want to resign ourselves to a rivalrous, individualist world or do we want to work toward solidarity and cooperation? Do we accept a world hurtling toward ecological devastation, a world in which the rich get richer and the poor get poorer? Or do we want to build a world in which people see the earth as "a shared inheritance, whose fruits are meant to benefit everyone" (LS 93)? Do we accept the dominant paradigm, geared to growth and profit, or believe that the economy should be shaped by other ideals, values, and criteria? Do we want a world of compulsive consumerism, or one that values a sober and satisfying life? Babylon or Jerusalem? A world of sacrifice or one of mercy, indifference or fraternity? And what does all this mean, for my own personal choices?

Let's go first to the smoking plains of Babylon. The earth around it is burning from rainforest clearances, fossil fuel extraction, and bush fires. It is a place of lavish wealth in the center, but surrounding it is grinding poverty, where "a constant flood of new products coexists with a tedious monotony" (LS 113). In this "free market," most people are out for themselves, but at the same time everybody is enslaved to the powerful. Who is there? What expressions are on their faces?

Now come closer and listen to Lucifer's instructions to the demons on how to tempt people away from God's plan by instilling a desire in them for *riches, honor,* and *pride*. Imagine it as a briefing in a large office space, complete with screens and presentation slides. Consider his arguments and inducements, and the suggestions made by the demons. What might they use to tempt you to focus on your own concerns? Imagine the demons (who, of course, do not look like demons) crowding round you, flattering you with enticing offers, offering you a path to power and mastery at the expense of the world around you. Have you ever been tempted in this way?

Next go to the plains of Jerusalem. Imagine an estate or farm or village, or perhaps a city, teeming with diversity and life but also peaceful and joyful. It is a humble and organic place that does not block out or suppress the natural world but lives in full partnership with it. How do people live there? What choices have they made? What are the expressions on their faces? Take time to look around.

As you draw closer, hear Jesus speaking to those he has called, inviting them to help everyone to desire spiritual poverty as opposed to riches, humiliation rather than honor, humility rather than pride.

Some of his followers come out to greet you and explain what this means by using the Beatitudes in Matthew chapter 5, and especially the third verse: "Blessed are the poor in spirit." They speak of detachment from the goods of this world, and other kinds of freedom they enjoy; they explain what it means to operate patiently and humbly, forgiving the slights of others, accepting when things do not go according to one's own plans. And they surprise you when they explain that this way of behaving is also key to the way they relate to the world around them, which is laid out in chapter 4 of *Laudato Si'*, and especially in paragraphs 222–227.

Together with the Two Standards and *Laudato Si'*, Jesus' famous parable of the prodigal and his brother (Luke 15:11–32) offers us a way of understanding ecological conversion in the early twenty-first century.

The father's estate is the place we have just imagined. It is an oasis of integral ecology, where creation and creatures are cared for and nurtured. The father passionately loves his sons and strives to give them all they need. But for the younger son, this is not enough. He burns with frustrated ambition, insecurity, and anxiety. He chafes at the limits of his garden world, and he despises it.

Desperate to prove himself and make a mark on the world, he asks the father to cash in his future inheritance, turning it into capital he can use now. Leaving the estate in search of opportunities, he ends up in a far-off land where loose regulations are a magnet for speculators and investors. He seeks wealth, success, independence; he wants to be respected and admired. And for a time, all this happens. Like young Giovanni Bernardone, he becomes a model for the desires of others. His clever investments and lavish living make him popular. At last he can stand out and above others. "Look at me, with all this that I've earned," he says. He feels important, the center of the world.

But then it all turns sour. The Gospel speaks of famine striking the land, but it might equally be a financial collapse or the outbreak of war or a pandemic that causes an economic shutdown and a cost-of-living crisis.

His wealth gone, the prodigal now wakes to the truth about the desires that had been driving him. Jesus makes clear in his telling of the parable that this takes time; the prodigal's reevaluation is radical. What triggers the rethink is less the sudden material poverty than the pain of the loneliness it has led to. His friends are gone. They desired him for what he desired: success and wealth. Perhaps he only valued them because they desired what he did. Being poor now, a failure in their eyes, he is no longer desired, and they have drifted away. In his heartache, the prodigal realizes that what he craved after all was love. He had confused love with admiration, and believed it had to be earned.

His value to others, it turns out, was determined by his price, which has fallen. And now he discovers what it means to live in the bottom of a world where price dictates value: the pigs on the farm where he finds work are fed before the farmhands because they can be sold in the market for more than his labor. Many people experience the labor market in this way. Flattered to be courted by employers, they thought they were special because they were promoted over others and singled out for praise and awards. But one day they are let go because shareholders demanded costs be cut so they could extract more dividends. Their worth, it turns out, was based on their price, and prices fluctuate with supply and demand.

The prodigal wakes up. He sees that he has been treated as a commodity and that this is how he has treated others. The pain he feels leads him to a second realization: we are not commodities and should not be treated as such. He now grasps what it means to live in a commodified world, where everything can be privatized and its value extracted and sold—as he did with his inheritance. He begins to see the repercussions of all this, not just on his fellow human creatures but on the whole of creation. In the midst of his introspection he asks himself how this was meant to be in the beginning, what the Creator intended. And at the moment he begins to think about the Creator, he becomes aware of the cry of the earth and the cry of the poor blending into one cry and calling out to him.

At this point he looks back on his family estate with new eyes: even the servants there were treated with respect. He grasps that what he had despised was not the estate but himself. Hope creeps back into his heart. He has forfeited all rights as a son, but perhaps he could return as a servant? He could work as one who demands nothing yet who serves the common good of the estate. As he imagines this, he is filled with a feeling of peace. He decides to return.

The father who scans the empty road for his returning son is Jesus' most famous totem of God's mercy waiting to overflow into hearts hardened by sacrifice. The father does not ask his son to pay for his errors and sins; all he cares is that his child has come to his senses and is back in the bosom of the family.

But the bitterness of the elder son shows how the paradigm persists, how hard it is to embrace the logic of gift and forgiveness. Both brothers are given the chance in Jesus' parable to move to a different way of thinking. But it is surely easier for the younger one to do so, for his broken heart has made space for the ecology of mercy.

POINT FOR REFLECTION

How have the "stoppages" in my own life led to a reevaluation?

SPIRITUAL EXERCISES, DAY 5 (WEEK 2)

Meditation on the Two Standards (SE 136–148)

- *Taking* the third chapter of *Querida Amazonia*, "The Ecological Dream," insert your belonging place instead of Amazonia in paragraphs 56–57, in order to hear its "cry" and to consider it as a theological locus. Spend time outside, and listen to creation speak.
- *Consider* the Meditation on the Two Standards in the light of the call to ecological conversion. Graces to ask for: "a knowledge of the deceits of the rebel chief and help to guard myself against them" and to know "the true life" exemplified by Jesus "and the grace to imitate Him" (SE 139).
- *Ponder: Laudato Si'*, chapter 4, 222–227, and *Laudate Deum*, especially chapters 2 and 6.
- *Imaginative contemplation:* What do I desire?

Contemplate-Discern-Propose

- *Contemplate:* Chapter 6 of *Laudato Si'*, especially 216–221. The parable of the prodigal and his brother (Luke 15:11–32).
- *Discern:* How is my own "ecological conversion"? Where are the resistances in me, and where am I being called and consoled?
- *Propose:* What can I do, both individually and in collaboration with others? Look up the *Laudato Si'* Action Platform for ideas. https://laudatosiactionplatform.org/

For many days we discussed the various aspects of this question, analyzing and weighing the relative merits and cogency of each argument, always allowing time for our customary practices of prayer, meditation and reflection. Finally, with the help of God, we came to a decision. . . . We continued in these and other deliberations for almost three months—from the latter part of Lent to the feast of John the Baptist—adhering to this same mode of procedure in our analysis and discussion of each issue, always proposing both sides of the question. By the feast of St. John, all our business was pleasantly concluded in a spirit of perfect harmony. But it was only by first engaging in prolonged vigils and prayers, with much expenditure of physical and mental energy that we resolved these problems and brought them to this happy conclusion.

—St. Ignatius

DAY SIX

Around the Common Table

*On the Call to Fraternity, and
to Build a Synodal Church*

Convocation in the Spirit

In an address to journalists in August 2023, Francis spoke of his dream of a synodal Church as "a grace which we all need in order to move forward," something the church can offer "a world so often incapable of making decisions, even when our very survival is at stake."

Francis was speaking on the eve of the first of two synod assemblies in Rome (October 2023 and October 2024) that concluded a process of consultation and listening to the people of God that had begun two years earlier, in October 2021.

The so-called synod on synodality had moved through various stages and levels, from parish and diocese to national and continental, involving reports, syntheses, and assemblies across the globe. It was the largest such exercise in the history of the Church, the most extensive listening operation ever carried out by a single institution, and the most significant event in the Catholic Church since the Second Vatican Council.

Francis told the journalists that this wasn't an exercise in introspection, but the opposite: a global act of self-transcendence, not just for the sake of the Church but for humanity, in which what was at stake was the very art of fraternal coexistence during a time of polarization and fragmentation.

> Precisely at this time, when there is so much talking and such little listening, when the notion of the common good risks being weakened, the entire Church has embarked on a journey to rediscover the word *together*. We must rediscover the word *together*. Walking *together*. Discussing *together*. Taking responsibility *together* for a communitarian discernment just as the first apostles did, which for us is prayer. This is synodality, which we would like to become part of our everyday culture. . . . We are trying to learn a new way of living relationships: listening to one another, hearing and following the voice of the Spirit. We have opened our doors, we have offered everyone the opportunity to participate, we have taken into account everyone's needs and suggestions. We want to contribute together to build the Church where everyone feels at home, where no one is excluded. That word of the Gospel that is so important: *everyone*. Everyone, everyone: there are no first, second or third class Catholics, no. All together. Everyone. That is the Lord's invitation.

In the decade of his pontificate Francis's conviction had grown that synodality was "what God was asking of the Church in the third millennium," as he put it in a famous speech in 2015. Synodality was a way of proceeding together and a way of making decisions that the Church practiced from its earliest days, when the apostles turned to the Holy Spirit to help them work out major questions that divided them. Recovering this spiritual art of communal discernment, which the early Jesuits in particular had practiced, has been a priority for him, the need ever more urgent in the face of powerful forces currently polarizing and tribalizing all of humanity, including the Church. Francis had linked a synodal Church and a fraternal world when he was elected on March 13, 2013. From the balcony of St. Peter's he spoke of the Church as "bishop and people together" on "a journey of fraternity, of love, of trust among us," before inviting everyone to pray "for the whole world, that there may be a great spirit of fraternity."

When he opened the synod assembly of October 4–29, 2023, in Rome, Francis made clear what the 365 church leaders gathered in Rome from across the world were not there to do. "We are not here to carry out a parliamentary meeting or plan of reformation," he said in his homily in St. Peter's Square, but "to be a Church that, with a glad heart, contemplates God's action and discerns the present." This assembly would do what the apostles and elders had first done when they gathered 20 years after Jesus' death and Resurrection, as described in chapter 15 of the Acts of the Apostles.

They saw then that God was doing something new, and sought to understand it and respond to it. Even though they were divided, they did not gather to decide between two parties, but to discern the Spirit's call. Likewise, the October 2023 gathering in Rome was not a gathering to settle differences over, for example, how to recognize women's leadership in the Church or the barriers to inclusion of various minorities. It was not a "political gathering," in Francis's words, but a "convocation in the Spirit." Its purpose was to listen deeply and to dialogue, to grow in unity with each other and with the Lord, "in order to look at today's challenges with his gaze." Changes might follow, as they did after the Council at Jerusalem—but only after a consensus became clear that this was the direction the Spirit was pointing.

The call to the Church to "become synodal" is Francis's bold response to the signs of our times. It was St. Paul VI who said that the Church in the west had lost the idea and habit of synodality which so characterized the Christian community in the first millennium. By this he meant the habit of discernment in common, of seeking the guidance of the Holy Spirit which Jesus had promised would lead the Church into the whole truth (John 16:13). Synodality is an attempt to take seriously the protagonism of the Spirit in the life of the Church. As Francis has often repeated, it is the Spirit who forms and leads the Church, who gathers up the baptized and sends them out, who pours out different gifts on all the believers for their mission—as prophets, healers, teachers, administrators and almsgivers (Romans 12:5–16). At the same time, it is the Spirit who harmonizes differences, not by suppressing them but creating a "bond of communion between dissimilar parts," as Francis put it in his opening assembly address, quoting Saint Basil of Caesarea.

The assembly of October 2023 used a new method and a format designed to capture the "new thing" the Spirit was doing. It was meant to enable listening, discernment, and participation, with plenty of time for prayer and silence. Rather than only bishops giving speeches in a theatre-style hall, as in previous synods, the Paul VI audience hall was cleared for 35 round tables at which sat not just bishops and cardinals but religious brothers and sisters, clergy and lay people, men and women, young and old. All took part as equals and were encouraged to speak freely. Both the wedding banquet-style layout and the method used aimed to encourage "the passage from listening to one another to listening to the Spirit" in the words of the assembly's general rapporteur, Cardinal Jean-Claude Hollerich.

The method was known as 'Conversation in the Spirit.' It was similar to the one used 500 years ago when the first Jesuits met to discern what the Lord was calling them to. After introductions came silent prayer. Then each of the ten or eleven in each group spoke in turn for a maximum of four minutes in response to a question. No discussion or responses were allowed at this point. Then there was more silent prayer, in which members pondered the "resonances" in their hearts and minds to what they had heard. Then came a second round, each person again contributing for three minutes on what had touched them or occurred to them in the first round, so allowing the group to see where the Spirit might be moving. Finally, after more silent prayer, in the third round a freer exchange of dialogue allowed the group to agree or disagree with each other, and to conclude together where there were convergences, divergences, or questions that need to be clarified. There was no attempt to force a false consensus, or negotiate compromises. The fruits of each group's discernment were then shared with the wider assembly. The following day, each group finalized their report in the light of what they had heard and reflected on.

The experience was transformative. People came to see what lay behind the beliefs or convictions involved in disagreements or different perspectives, and to understand and respect others' context and motivations. But they also saw beyond the surface of the ideas themselves, to become aware of the spirits involved: where the good Spirit was enabling a new awareness or clarity, or, conversely, where someone might not be offering their view as a gift to be shared but as a power-play, seeking to impose or block. People learned, too, to spot these contrary spirits in themselves, to see how much they were called to conversion. As those involved learned the "grammar of synodality," they came to understand more deeply what it means to be part of a body larger than each of them, in which the Spirit has been poured out on all. They experienced something of how God's saving, unifying power works within the Church.

This way of proceeding is hard for modern western democracies to understand. We have become used to differences being settled or resolved through debates and votes: one side wins, the other loses. It is a power game, in which rhetoric, strategy, and all kinds of persuasion (including bribes and threats) are brought into play. Rather than uniting the body, polarization is deployed as a political instrument, rubbing the wounds of indignation and grievance to foster resentment of the other. "Post-truth" politics is waged as a war of competing narratives between different groups each claiming to possess the truth. Differences are not transcended, but sharpened and deepened. Even though democracies came into being to contain differences peacefully, these polarizing dynamics too often spill out into violence, even war. The deeper our divisions, the harder it is to meet the challenges humanity faces. Little wonder Francis in *Fratelli Tutti* sees fraternity as the task of our time.

In recovering the Christian tradition of synodality, Francis is asking the Church to go in the opposite direction, to learn how unity and fraternity can be built from the ground up, by opening to God's saving action, and engaging in a common search for the Spirit who will lead us together into the truth. It means, first, putting aside for a time our own view, our own way of thinking, in order to make room for the other's. Second, it means being attentive to the voices outside our experience, especially the often prophetic voices from the margins, and to be aware of the resonances that listening to others arouses within us. Third, it means allowing space for difficult questions to be raised and clarified, but not trying to settle differences too soon by imposing answers or solutions. Rather than "winners" or "losers", the challenge is to create processes that lead to consensus over time, in prayer and peace. In this way, when decisions are ready to be taken, all feel they have been involved in the making of the decision through consultation and discernment.

This does not mean that truth is decided by some kind of democratic process, as the synod's critics claim. Neither Christian doctrine nor Catholic tradition—the papacy, the Eucharist, and so on—are under discussion in synods. But how these are lived out and expressed, and what new forms of life are needed for the new conditions and forms of apostolate of today's world, need constantly to be discerned. As Francis reminds us, tradition is a living, dynamic reality, constantly growing and developing; divine revelation is not just what happened in the past but is an ongoing encounter with God's love and God's will in the present. In its ministries and mechanisms, its structures and its internal culture, the Church has always looked very different from one age to the next, as it becomes more fully what it is called to be over time.

Synodality means that an increasingly global, diverse Church can move ahead to receive that ongoing revelation, without rupturing the body. Synodal processes require patience and humility. But their fruit is not just in the quality of the decisions taken, but in the deeper communion they bring about. Because of the action of the Spirit, differences are not destructive of unity but help create it. Rather than fuel division, contrasting viewpoints become dynamic and generative. We can experience both the presence of the Lord and the beauty of belonging, and can say, with the apostles and the elders of the Council at Jerusalem: "It has seemed good to the Holy Spirit and to us . . ." (Acts 15:28)

At the conclusion of the October 2023 assembly the members voted overwhelmingly to approve the synthesis report, which says that "synodality is the future of the Church." Today's reflections are to help us undertake that journey of synodal conversion, both individually and in community. First, we look at the attachments and obstacles that keep us locked in our limited standpoints. Then we consider how we can be "apostles of fraternity" in the polarized environments of our time. Finally, we look at the virtues and mindsets needed for synodality by considering Ignatius's guidelines for discerning spirits and "thinking with the Church."

Fraternity is the sign of the presence of the kingdom of God among us. It is known in the Gospel by a banquet, a feast, and a shared table. What matters at that table is not just that all are *fed* but that all *belong*. As Francis said in Chile in 2018, "Recognizing that the poor, the naked, the sick, prisoners and the homeless have the dignity to sit at our table, to feel 'at home' among us, to feel part of a family . . . is the sign that the kingdom of heaven is in our midst." This is the image of the culture of encounter that Francis uses in his second, "cultural" dream for Amazonia:

> Starting from our roots, let us sit around the common table, a place of conversation and of shared hopes. In this way our differences, which could seem like a banner or a wall, can become a bridge. Identity and dialogue are not enemies. Our own cultural identity is strengthened and enriched as a result of dialogue with those unlike ourselves. Nor is our authentic identity preserved by an impoverished isolation (QA 37).

POINT FOR REFLECTION

How do you feel about the Church "becoming synodal"?

Three Attachments

The "Three Classes of Men" (SE 149–157) are about attachments that trap us in rivalry. Ignatius tells us that each of them has acquired ("not entirely as they should have, for the love of God") a large sum of money; all three want to free themselves of "the burden arising from the attachment" to it (ES 150). Note that the question is not *what to do* with the money but *being free to decide* what to do with it. It may be right to give away the money, or keep it, or use it in a particular way; the question needs to be discerned by each of them. But as long as they are *inordinately attached* to the money, discernment cannot happen. They are not free to know and follow God's will because they have already organized their lives to hold on to what they have. And as Jesus said, you cannot serve two masters (see Matthew 6:24).

An unhealthy attachment is a power over us. We are possessed by what we possess. Fearing to lose what we think we cannot live without, we cannot "come out of ourselves" to receive from God what will give us life. We may have and enjoy many things, but, as the Principle and Foundation reminds us, they should help us use them for God's glory. So the key lies in what we *first* desire, to whom we *first* belong. Is the Kingdom the pearl of great price, for which I am willing to give up pearls of lesser value? Do I want to follow God's will, as Jesus does, or to bend God to the shackles of my own unfree desires?

The grace we ask for in this prayer is the former: we *want* to be generous, we *want* to be open, so that we might choose what is *more* for the glory of God, in order better to serve the kingdom as well as my own salvation and fulfillment (ES 152).

In Bergoglio's talks to the Argentine Jesuits (and later to the Spanish bishops), he named the "spirit of sufficiency" as the core attachment that stops us from giving of ourselves. This is the spirit that holds back the wealthy young man in Mark 10:17–22, despite his moral integrity and his heart's restless desire for "more."

Bergoglio identified three areas in particular. The first he called "my hegemony, which leads me to confuse the part with the whole." It is to believe that my way of seeing, my way of doing, is the only viable way, and that others need to get with my program. The second he called "my conscience, when we defend it as an attachment apart from the conscience of the faithful." In the Church, this involves embracing an "isolated conscience" above the people of God, in particular dogmatic positions (traditionalism, progressivism, etc.) that claim a monopoly on holiness and truth. A third attachment is to cling to power and comfort, leading us jealously to safeguard our freedom, time, resources, and ideas, or avoid making choices or dealing with tensions. This is the temptation of irenicism—peace at any price, the avoidance of conflict.

"It will do us good to remember," Bergoglio told the Spanish bishops, "that every attachment undermines the unity of the Church, creating division in order to spread confusion." What isolates us from the body, he added, "is always something petty that we want to keep for ourselves."

If the spirit of sufficiency makes us stingy, the *magis*—desiring what is *more* for God's glory—is the antidote that opens our hearts. The *magis* leads us out to be bold, magnanimous, and creative, to desire to act, as in the well-known Jesuit motto *Ad Majorem Dei Gloriam*, "for God's greater glory."

The *magis* does not mean "more" in a crude sense of doing or achieving more, as if everything depends on us and our efforts. It is more like falling in love, when we think more of the needs of our beloved than of our own, desiring to do what they want rather than what we want. In the spiritual life the *magis* invites us to focus on the major task of God's kingdom rather than on our own personal empire. It is to search for a "more universal good," having "a heart open to the whole world," as we read in the title of chapter 4 of *Fratelli Tutti*. In his talks to the Jesuits, Bergoglio stressed two particular dimensions of the *magis*: responsibility and creativity.

Responsibility is when the disciple is called to "take charge of the apostolic body." It is to take up a mission as reconciler, peacemaker, and builder of unity. This disciple neither fuels division nor stands aloof from tension and conflict but initiates processes that open people to the unifying action of the Spirit. She endures conflict, yes, but does so in ways that resolve that conflict, thereby making it "a link in the chain of a new process" (EG 227).

Creativity is when the disciple seeks to *cooperate with* the grace God is offering in situations of conflict or crisis, and to conceive of ways forward, through discernment. As Bergoglio puts it, "The creativity of the Christian needs to show forth in opening up new horizons, opening windows, opening transcendence towards God and towards people."

Jesus' cure of the man born blind in chapter 9 of John's Gospel shows the path to this responsibility and creativity, and what prevents it. Read through the lens of the "Three Classes," the story shows how to move beyond our attachments to embrace the unity God is waiting to show us.

The first kind of people in the story are the Pharisees. They cling to prejudices that protect them from reality because they fear losing their position and authority. Their blindness, typical of the powerful and privileged, afflicts religious authorities who cling to their status as gatekeepers of the goods of God. The Pharisees demand to know what has happened to the man born blind, but only so they can confirm their prejudgment, or prejudice. They see Jesus as a rival. A miracle, should it be demonstrated, threatens their attachments. Their persistent, angry questioning reveals their fears and unease.

The second kind of people are the blind man's parents and neighbors. They know the man was born blind and he can now see as a result of Jesus curing him. Yet, for fear of the crowd and the Pharisees, they will not stand up for the truth as they know it. They cling to their comfort and a quiet life, keep their heads down, deflect the questions, and seek peace at any price.

The third kind of people—very few in this episode, and usually a minority in society—are those who embrace the truth they come to see, and are led by its consequences to take action, whatever the cost. Some Pharisees in the Gospel passage begin along this path, daring to ask how, if Jesus were a sinner, he could perform such signs

(John 9:16). But it is the man born blind who in the Gospel embodies this journey into truth. He lacks status or learning, yet he can "see" the deeper realities at stake. He is like the heroes Francis speaks of in *Fratelli Tutti* who "determine respectfully to promote truthfulness, aside from personal interest" (FT 202).

As all hell breaks loose around the man born blind, he sticks to the evidence. Stubbornly, based on his direct experience, he gives truthful answers to hostile questions, even daring to point to the self-serving contradictions in which the Pharisees have wrapped themselves. At that point the Pharisees, indignant, drive him out. There, outside the community, alone and shunned, Jesus encounters him, reveals himself, and invites him to follow.

What happens afterward can only be imagined in prayer. Yet we sense that the man with new sight will be at the service of truth and of unity. He will follow Jesus, who "came to strengthen and deepen the bonds of belonging, of the people to God and to each other" (LUD 105). He will help build a people, working to a new horizon of the common good, renewing bonds through dialogue (AL 136–141). He will create "processes of encounter, processes that build a people capable of accepting differences" (FT 217). In enduring contempt and hostility for the sake of the truth, he shows himself to be like Jesus, who "after insults and outrages, He might die on the Cross, and all this for me" (SE 116).

The *magis* of fraternity is a willingness to endure hostility without retaliating, to be patient when people are rude to you, to seek the horizon of unity at all costs. This is the virtue of kindness, which is no "superficial bourgeois virtue," says Francis in *Fratelli Tutti*. In our post-truth media environment, with its clashing ideologies and furious disputes, kindness "opens new paths where hostility and conflict would burn all bridges" (FT 224).

POINT FOR REFLECTION

Which tempts me more: to fuel polarization or to paper over conflict?

Apostles of Fraternity

With the loss of civility and the breakdown of public discourse, the call to Christ's disciples to become apostles of fraternity has become pressing. Technology has brought us together in whole new ways, yet in other ways it has driven us apart.

It can seem at times that truth is no longer a common good, available to everyone, but has become a commodity for commercial or political exploitation. Politicians, corporations, even states have discovered the power of disseminating half-truths to whip up anxieties and play on grievances. In *Fratelli Tutti* Francis describes this "feverish exchange of opinions on social networks" as no more than "parallel monologues"—people shouting past each other (FT 200).

If technology plays its part in amplifying and sharpening these trends, Francis sees behind them a spiritual malaise, one born of the anguish of nonbelonging. Social, economic, and cultural shifts have caused people to feel uprooted, thrust aside, and left behind. Their anxiety and indignation are tinder awaiting a flame—and there is no shortage of politicians waiting to act as arsonists. Behind a "public arena increasingly dominated by the beleaguered self—anxious, controlling, quick to take offense, self-justifying" Francis sees "a fragility of selfhood, a loss of roots, in which security is found in discrediting others through narratives that let us feel righteous and give us reasons for silencing others" (LUD 76).

Against this background, a synodal Church is called to be a counter-sign, its members committed to walking together with others to build the common good. It means the ability, in the words of the working document of the October 2023 synod, "to be agents of reconciliation and artisans of peace," especially in places marked by deep conflict. To be an apostle of fraternity in such an environment demands discernment. "Ideas can be *discussed*," Francis has frequently observed, "but vital situations have to be *discerned*." To see a disagreement or conflict as *only* about ideas is to fail to recognize the deeper spiritual forces at stake and to realize that "fallacious reasonings, subtleties and continual deceptions" are the *modus operandi* of the evil spirit (SE 329). Discernment is more difficult in a climate of mutual accusation and inflammatory rhetoric. But it is even more essential. There is a need to step back, disengage, and take stock in prayer and reflection.

One of the strategies of the bad spirit is to persuade us that in every conflict there is a contradiction that demands we choose a side—the side, obviously, of what is good and right. Ignatius's second-week discernment rules warn us that the bad spirit can assume the guise of light (SE 332). It is all too easy to be seduced by appeals to the good, the true, and the righteous. When we charge into a situation in defense of the truth, we can often find ourselves fighting under the banner of the bad spirit. Which is why, in his historic 2015 address to the joint session of the United States Congress, Francis warned against the temptation of a "simplistic reductionism which sees only good or evil; or, if you will, the righteous and sinners." For, he warned, "in the attempt to be freed of the enemy without, we can be tempted to feed the enemy within."

The first conversion we need is to the kind of patience Jesus describes in his story of the landowner who tells his servants not to rush in to pull up the weeds in his wheat field. He orders them instead to let crop and darnel grow together, and to divide them at harvest-time, when it is clear which is which (Matthew 13:24–30). An impulsive, aggressive stance too early puts too much faith in our own efforts and ability, said Francis in a July 2023 homily, whereas "the purification of the heart and the definitive victory over evil are essentially God's work."

This patient holding back is especially important in contexts of polarization. Francis showed his wisdom in this regard in August 2018, when a disgruntled former church official launched a ferocious attack on him. Archbishop Carlo Maria Viganò claimed Francis had covered up a high-profile abuse case earlier that summer, and demanded his resignation. By the time he was onboard the flight back to Rome, speculation was feverish and the air thick with accusation. Yet the pope chose to say nothing, instead inviting journalists to research the matter and draw their own conclusions. "It's an act of faith," he said. The journalists got to work, and within days the "Testimony" was revealed to be a mélange of half-truths and downright falsehoods. Not only were its central claims exposed as a lie, but Viganò's own dubious motives and psychology were laid bare.

At daily Mass from his Santa Marta residence in that fall of 2018, Francis continued not to refer directly to the accusations, offering instead guidance in discernment. By means of his silence, he said, "Jesus wins against the devil who sows lies in the heart." The lesson was clear: do not argue with people trying to polarize, and do not be taken in by false contradictions, but allow the spirits to reveal themselves.

Francis contrasted the meekness and steadiness of truth with the hysterical accusations of the "Great Accuser." The latter points to people's sins and failings in order to create scandal, yet the claims burn out quickly, like a camera flash. But he also indicated the difference in *effect*. Whereas the Spirit of Truth—gentle, humble, but firm—unites the body, "the father of lies, the accuser, the devil, acts to destroy the unity of a family, of a people."

The second conversion we need is made clear later in the Gospel, when Jesus warns his followers that he comes to bring not peace but a sword (see Matthew 10:34–11:1). The peace Christ brings is not the peace that comes from deflecting or denying tension and disagreement. The bad spirit's alternative strategy is to persuade us that there is *no* conflict when there *is*. This is the spirit that seeks to paper over divisions, reach for a hasty compromise, and when all else fails, settle the matter by a vote. This path of irenicism or relativism—"peace at any price"—proves expensive in the long run because it denies the division and thereby embeds it. Irenicism sterilizes differences, preventing the Spirit from acting to make them fruitful versus *in unum* (in the direction of unity). This is polite coexistence that evades the tension, just as with the second "Classes of Men" in Ignatius's exercise.

Francis asks us to discern disagreements. Are we dealing with a contraposition or a genuine contradiction? A contradiction is disjunctive; it demands we choose between truth and falsehood, reality and fantasy, good and evil. But most disagreements involve a contraposition, that is, a tension between two poles that are striving for unity and integration. The tension in a contraposition is productive; it calls for a process that allows the differences to enter into dialogue, which in turn allows something new to be opened up. Enabling and hosting such processes are what Francis describes in *Evangelii Gaudium* 227 as the *third way*, the way of the peacemaker.

Ignatius, he noted, did not fear disagreement, but rather "self-sufficiency"—a closure to the Spirit—which he saw as the real cause of disunity. Either to fuel conflict (polarization) or to deny it (relativism) is a form of closure to reality. The first is the self-sufficiency of those who already believe they possess the answers; the second case is the self-sufficiency of those who deny the conflict and avoid it. The third way, Jesus' way, is to call us into an openness to the truth, and thereby to grow. "I like to think," Francis says in *Let Us Dream*, "that we do not possess the truth so much as the truth possesses us, constantly attracting us by means of beauty and goodness" (LUD 54). Of course we do not undertake this journey as blank slates. We have the sure foundation of teaching and tradition to guide us, as well as our knowledge and reason. But these are always incomplete; there should always be an element of insufficiency in our thinking that leaves room for the Spirit's action. As Francis reminds us, "The Church's understanding and beliefs have expanded and consolidated over time in openness to the Spirit" (LUD 57). In each age the Spirit reveals new things in what is handed down over the ages, like the householder in Matthew 13:51–53. We need the humility to believe in the promise of Jesus to his disciples that over time the "Spirit . . . will guide you into all the truth" (John 16:13). It is a constant, evolving revelation.

The peacemakers are those who enable a "new process" (EG 227) that opens us to the guidance of the Spirit. It is a process that creates space for deep listening and dialogue. Those who take part are willing to learn from one another, receive one another's gifts, and be receptive to the new horizons offered by the Spirit. The hoped-for result, Francis says in *Querida Amazonia,* is that "conflict is overcome at a higher level, where each group can join the other in a new reality, while remaining faithful to itself" (QA 104–105).

In both *Querida Amazonia* and *Let Us Dream*, Francis uses the metaphor of "overflow" to describe this fruitfulness. It is when a group comes to recognize "a greater gift that God is offering" and embrace a new way of seeing that creates peace. It is an "overflow" in two senses. Like a river bursting its banks, it transcends the narrow channels of our present ways of seeing. And it is an overflow in the sense of Psalm 23, when our cup spills over with the grace the Good Shepherd gives us.

Such overflows happen above all, says Francis in *Let Us Dream*, "at moments of openness, fragility and humility, when the ocean of His love bursts the dams of our self-sufficiency, and so allows for a new imagination of the possible" (LUD 80).

POINT FOR REFLECTION

Can I think of a time when what I saw as a contradiction turned out to be a fruitful contraposition?

Thinking with the Church

Becoming a "wholly synodal Church," declared Francis in 2015, in one of the most important speeches of his pontificate, is what "God expects of the Church of the third millennium." A synodal Church, he said, "is a Church which listens. . . . The faithful People, the College of Bishops, the Bishop of Rome: all listening to each other; and all listening to the Holy Spirit."

Synodality is less a program to be carried out or way of making decisions so much as it is "a style to incarnate," as Francis told Catholic Action in 2021. It means "dialogue, discussion, research—but with the Spirit." It is not enough to *know about* synodality. The call is to *be* synodal. That means learning the mindset and habits that build communion in the Church and fraternity in society. And it means decision-making that incorporates spiritual discernment.

Discernment begins by listening to the experience of ordinary people whose faith wisdom is the fruit of the Spirit poured out on all the baptized. Through gatherings in which all may speak and be heard, we discover and receive the gifts that the Spirit has poured into the hearts of Christ's disciples. These are gifts that have been given us in order to help us serve others, and so build up the Church and God's kingdom on earth.

A synodal consciousness comes from the sharing and receiving of these gifts and the joy of recognizing where the Spirit is at work in the lives of people and in the Church. It also comes from realizing that these insights indicate the future paths for the Church to follow, and the changes that will be required.

Discernment takes seriously the promise Jesus made to his disciples when he told them that he would not leave them orphans but would send his Spirit to lead them. Discernment embodies the truth that the Holy Spirit is in charge of the Church and therefore that opposing spirits are also at work. Discernment means that differences are not resolved by power but by openness to a wisdom that transcends particular individuals or groups. Discernment involves a sincere search for God's will.

Synodal processes are full of ups and downs, highs and lows, temptations and distractions. These are signs that the good spirit is at work; otherwise, Francis says, the bad spirit wouldn't bother to attack and distract. The spirits involved need to be examined in order to bring to the surface personal or group attachments to self-serving agendas or hidden motivations.

Ignatius's various "Rules" at the end of the *Exercises*—for discernment of spirits (SE 313–336) and for thinking with the Church (SE 352–370)—are a wonderful resource for developing the wisdom and mindset we need for synodality. By "Rules" Ignatius meant points to keep in mind rather than regulations in the juridical sense; nowadays we might call them guidelines.

The "Rules for Thinking with the Church" are frequently overlooked by those giving the *Exercises* because they clearly belong to another age. Ignatius wrote them when Europe was split by the Reformation. Yet they are arguably more relevant now, in our age of institutional crisis and division, than ever before. As Francis told a 2016 meeting of Jesuits in Rome, Ignatius wrote them in response to an anti-ecclesial spirit, "in order to open ways in which the Spirit could work in his own time."

Ignatius, too, lived in an era of polarization within the Church. He saw that some ways of seeking to change the Church did not come from the Spirit: they slowed or distracted from the real reform by dividing and weakening the body. His concern, like Francis's now, was to enable change with a good spirit (that is, humbly, open to grace). That means enabling reform that flows from love, from a sense of belonging to the Church as Christ's body. The *Rules* are about learning to put the common good of the Church first, and seeing ourselves as part of the body. As described by St. Paul in his Letter to the Philippians (Philippians 2:1–5), this means being able to think *with* the Church, to take responsibility for it as Christ's instrument on earth.

The first rule (SE 353) is the key to the rest. Ignatius asks us to "put aside all judgment of our own" to be "ever ready and prompt to obey" the Church. Open, humble listening (the Latin root of the word *obey* is *ab-audire*, "to listen") to the Spirit requires suspending our prejudgments. When we prejudge either negatively or positively, we apply filters; we close our minds to what others are saying or we swallow what they say uncritically. In a synodal process we should "speak boldly and listen humbly," as Francis famously told the synod of bishops in 2014. Speaking boldly (*parrhesia*) means not hesitating to speak up and name the realities we see. But listening humbly means being receptive to what others say and allowing what is true and of God to resonate with us. Choosing to listen in this way gives value to Christ's body and our commitment to it.

Rule 13 is notorious in urging us to "hold fast to the following principle: What seems to me white, I will believe black if the hierarchical Church so defines." Ignatius goes on to explain what he means by this: "For I must be convinced that in both Christ and the Church 'one Spirit holds sway, which governs and rules for the salvation of souls.'" In the light of synodality and the practice of discernment in common this is not, after all, so controversial, but flows from the first rule. The Church is led by the one Spirit. Where an authentic mutual listening and discernment of spirits has taken place, are we not called to obey the result?

The results of those processes may not be ones I hoped for or agree with. But does this mean my view is superior to the wisdom of the Church? Do I believe that the discernment of the body is inferior to my own discernment? Francis warns in *Let Us Dream* that disappointment and a sense of defeat can be a sign that "you come wanting to achieve something, and when you didn't get it, you feel deflated." This in turn may indicate that "you remain trapped within your desires, rather than allowing yourself to be touched by the grace on offer" (LUD 92).

The other rules give us a list of practices and traditions in the Church to be praised. In his time just as much as in ours, the Church was the site of spiritual combat where corruption and abuse were present; Ignatius more than anyone knew the need of reform. But he also knew how the baby can get thrown out with the bathwater, and that too much focus on the sin and failure of others—and our own sense of righteousness in response—can corrupt us. So he asks us to begin by recognizing the good and the gifts we have received in and through the Church, through its teaching, its councils, its saints, but also its laws and edicts and commandments. As Rule 9 puts it, we must "be on the alert to find reasons to defend them, and by no means in order to criticize them."

In fostering belonging and unity, gratitude is a good place to start. In giving thanks for particular people or places in the Church that have cared for me and helped me grow, I can make my own list of the ways that the Church has inspired, encouraged, and formed me. And through the list I can realize that, for all its faults and failings and need of change, the Church has been, and remains for most of us, the primary means of our living out the gift of our belonging to God.

POINT FOR REFLECTION

How is my own "thinking with the Church?"

SPIRITUAL EXERCISES, DAY 6 (WEEK 2)

Meditation on The Three Classes of Men (SE 149–158)

- *Read: Evangelii Gaudium* 217–237 and *Fratelli Tutti* chapters 4 and 6. How do you feel about being a "missionary of fraternity," pursuing "contemplative fraternity," and working to build fraternity in your belonging place?
- *Grace to ask for:* "To choose what is more for the glory of his Divine Majesty and the salvation of my soul" (SE 152). (We could add here a desire to be free to serve the cause of unity; to choose responsibility for the body or place I belong to; and the gift of creativity to discern, in order to open up new processes of encounter and dialogue.)
- *Learning to discern:* SE 328–336, LUD 61–2; Francis's fourteen catecheses on discernment at General Audiences (September 7, 2022–December 14, 2022).
- *Scripture:* Mark 10:17–22; John 9.

Contemplate-Discern-Propose

- *Contemplate:* The mindset and attitudes for synodality in the Council of Jerusalem (Acts 15), LUD 81–94, and Ignatius's "Rules for Thinking with the Church" (SE 352–370).
- *Discern:* Using Ignatius's second-week rules for discernment of spirits, what might be the signs of the Spirit in a synodal meeting? How would you know?
- *Propose:* Looking at the synthesis report of the October 2023 synod ('A synodal Church in Mission' at synod.va), consider: How might synodality change how I organize, plan, and hold meetings in my parish or religious community? How could I use synodal methods to foster processes that allow tensions to become creative rather than generate conflict?

Ignatius, describing his experience of mercy in these comparative terms—the more he failed the Lord, the more the Lord reached out in giving him his grace—released the life-giving power of mercy which we, many times, dilute with our abstract formulations and legalistic conditions. The Lord who looks at us with mercy and chooses us, sends us out to bring with all its effectiveness, that same mercy to the poorest, to sinners, to those discarded people, and those crucified in the present world, who suffer injustice and violence. Only if we experience this healing power first-hand in our own wounds, as people and as a body, will we lose the fear of allowing ourselves to be moved by the immense suffering of our brothers and sisters, and will we hasten to walk patiently with our people, learning from them the best way of helping and serving them.

—Pope Francis

The Triumph of Failure

*On Touching Christ's Wounds,
and the Power of Patience*

To Suffer With

After the feeding of the four thousand, the cure of a blind man at
Bethsaida, and Peter's Spirit-filled declaration of faith in Jesus as the
Messiah, the eighth chapter of Mark's Gospel turns suddenly somber.
"Then he began to teach them that the Son of Man must undergo
great suffering, and be rejected by the elders, the chief priests, and the
scribes, and be killed, and after three days rise again. He said all this
quite openly" (Mark 8:31–32).

The mood continues to darken. Again in chapters 9 and 10 of
Mark, Jesus details what will happen. Peter is appalled. The others
do not understand. Jesus has until now manifested so spectacularly
his healing power and goodness, demonstrating that he is the Son of
the living God. Why would he allow himself to become a victim of
human power and degradation?

The healings and miracles are rare now, and soon cease. Hostility
to Jesus grows. Jesus begins to spend more time with his bewildered
apostles to prepare them for what is to come. He wants to teach them
about the paradoxes that they cannot fully grasp at this moment: that

the one ready to lose his life saves it; that the power of God is known in radical service; and that obedience to God's will requires that we accept suffering and forgive those who inflict it on us.

Even for us who are alive two thousand years after the Resurrection, this "way" set forth by Jesus is not readily grasped. Only when we look suffering in the eye, as Jesus did, trusting in God, does it begin to take on meaning. We know that with that kind of trust, suffering can transform us, and our world. We can allow the Cross to "work." But let's admit that it is not easy to have confidence in a power that is so obviously vulnerable.

Jesus is not just telling his disciples what will happen. As it now dawns on them, he is also asking them to follow him down the same path. If the first part of Mark's Gospel is Jesus showing the *meaning* of the kingdom of God, the second part is Jesus preparing them to *enter* it. The *Exercises* move along the same path: from the *purgative* (recognizing our sins) in Week 1 and the *illuminative* (understanding, hearing, and following Christ) in Week 2, we come to the *unitive* in Weeks 3 and 4. From now on, we are invited not only to contemplate and imitate Christ but to join ourselves to him, to share in his suffering and his glory.

To do this we must above all find space and quiet for depth of silence. Only in silence can our imagination and feelings receive the mystery of God's great mercy. When Ignatius asks us to consider how Jesus suffers cruelly, he asks us to suffer *with* Jesus and *for* Jesus. See how "the divinity hides itself" as evil appears to triumph, he tells us (SE 196). See that Jesus does all this "for my sins." What might I do and suffer for *him*? (SE 197).

There is an apostolic purpose to this. In sharing Christ's suffering, we are better able to confront the temptations we face after the graces we received during Week 2. Then we embraced Jesus' call to build God's kingdom, and offered to suffer with him. Now is the testing and deepening of that call, the time we choose *his* way and make it *our* way. Now is the time we choose to embrace the truth about life and humanity that Jesus from the Cross wishes to teach us.

What is that truth? It is the Principle and Foundation: the reason for which I exist. A flourishing human life is not found in the pursuit of pleasure or in fleeing from pain, or in obtaining power and success to make us invulnerable. We flourish in service when we belong to others through loving them.

In following Christ and his way, we choose to accept this reality, to live out of this truth. But we are fragile, and we vacillate. Ignatius knows that having made that choice, at least in our minds, the temptation to flee the consequences of that choice will be great. Faced with necessary suffering—suffering that is God's will for us, necessary suffering that we must undergo in order to grow—we will be distracted. The weapon of distraction the enemy of our human nature will deploy is repugnance of suffering, which causes us to flee from the reality of need and pain and retreat back into ourselves.

Repugnance of suffering is Satan's biggest achievement. It is his most effective tactic and the source of his continuing power over us. It lies behind human indifference to the pain of others, and contempt for the poor, and the endless distractions from pain our consumerist lifestyle throws at us. All of these expressions of indifference, these distractions, rely on illusory narratives that tell an untruthful story about humans. They are stories we tell ourselves so that our consciences remain untroubled.

"How is it that we allow throwaway culture, in which millions of men and women are worth nothing compared to economic goods, how is it that we allow this culture to dominate our lives, our cities, our way of life?" Francis asked in his video message for the prayer intention of September 2023. Peering off to one side of the screen, away from the camera, he joked that "our necks are going to get stiff from looking the other way so we don't have to see this situation."

Yet repugnance of suffering is also, as a result of the Cross, Satan's blind spot and the place of his unmasking. In embracing humiliation and pain and ultimately death, Jesus shows definitively where God stands in relation to suffering. Seemingly "lesser" human beings from whom the world recoils—"thrown away" people like the disabled, the disfigured, the disenfranchised, the sinners, the failures, the forgotten, the abused and the oppressed, the widows and trafficked children and despised foreigners—all of these are *fully human* beings. They are children of God, beloved by God. Every one of them has been endowed with the inherent dignity God gives to his creatures. Each has a cry God has heard and on whose behalf he is acting, calling us to give shelter and welcome to those living in inhuman conditions.

Since God has gone into the very depths of human degradation, the satanic narratives may continue to cast a spell. But their lie is shattered.

In choosing to suffer with Jesus—which is the choice Ignatius invites us to make in today's exercise—we join ourselves to that divine action. We choose not to turn away, either from Jesus' horror and pain or from the pain and horror of every person's suffering. We cannot control what will befall us or what will cross our path. But we can choose to accept it in the manner of courage and obedience modeled by Christ who, when he was offered a chance to save himself, countered with an offering of his very self (Luke 23:35, 37, 39).

Christ's Passion involves suffering of every kind: of the body, of the soul, and of the spirit. The cruelty of the physical pain—the slaps, whips, thorns, and nails—is only one aspect of the more profound psychological humiliation of being betrayed, mocked, isolated, and scorned as an impostor and blasphemer. Jesus is jeered at by crowds who once flocked to him for favors. Now they scream to have him punished.

He is put to death by political authorities who carry out the sentence even though they know he is innocent. He is betrayed by religious leaders who manufacture justifications for his murder. Every institution fails. Every law is broken. Every possibility of justice is cast aside. As the machine of power turns against him and moves to crush him, everyone flees. Jesus is forsaken and abandoned by almost everyone he loves. Those who promised to stand with him deny him and escape from him.

Jesus even experiences the loss of the one certainty that sustained him, which was that God his Father was close. On the Cross, he suffers a searing moment of desolation: *God, my God, why have you forsaken me?* As Francis put it on Palm Sunday in 2020, "Jesus experienced total abandonment in a situation he had never before experienced in order to be one with us in everything." Jesus did this, he added, "in order not to leave us prey to despair, so as to stay at our side forever."

The grace we seek for this day is "sorrow, compassion and shame because the Lord is going to His suffering for my sins" (SE 193). Our desire is to experience "sorrow with Christ in sorrow, anguish with Christ in anguish, tears and deep grief because of the great anguish Christ endures for me" (SE 203). Francis suggests also asking for the grace "to love Jesus in his abandonment and to love Jesus in the abandoned all around us," and for "the grace to see and acknowledge the Lord who continues to cry out in them."

Let us at the same time contemplate how the Lord cries out in his *nonhuman* creatures. "The whole of creation is a manifestation of the love of God," Francis wrote in his 2022 teaching on the liturgy, *Desiderio Desideravi*, "and from when that same love was manifested in its fullness in the Cross of Jesus, all of creation was drawn toward it." How does this drawing to the Cross happen in the Passion? What is creation's role?

As we read the Passion narratives let us pay attention to the crowing cock, the thorns and reeds, the vinegar, the rocks that split and make a tomb, the nard and the water, the bread and the wine, the wood of the Cross, and the eclipse of the light of the world. You will notice other elements of creation, twisted and manipulated by raw power, call to us. Does creation not also mediate God's presence? Can we hear the echo of Jesus' cry, and the cries of the poor, in the cries of the earth?

POINT FOR REFLECTION

What does it mean to choose to suffer with another?

The Baited Hook

How does the Cross "triumph"? How does Christ's submission to his Father's purpose bring about our salvation, and loosen Satan's grip?

In "Word and Silence," one of his most powerful essays from his "desert period" in the early 1990s, Bergoglio describes the strategy of Jesus in terms used by the Greek fathers in the first centuries of Christianity as a ruse or trap laid by God for Satan.

This tactic involved no deceit or dishonesty. As René Girard points out, God's "trick" only seems so because of "the inability of the prince of this world to understand the divine love." The Cross unmasks the mystique of power, in other words, in a way that power itself cannot conceive. As St. Paul says, "None of the rulers of this age understood [the wisdom of God]; for if they had they would not have crucified the Lord of glory" (1 Corinthians 2:7–9). Jesus achieves victory over

Satan, Girard writes, "through a renunciation of violence so complete that violence can rage to its heart's content without realizing that by so doing, it reveals what it must conceal."

What the Resurrection will bring about is an unveiling of the way evil works. The self-deception and false justification of violence are that it is somehow good, or necessary, or demanded by God. Yet after the Resurrection, Jesus' followers will record, exactly and truthfully, what happened: Jesus, the Son of God, was the wholly innocent victim of self-interested power. The justifications shown in the Passion accounts—that he was a criminal, a blasphemer, a threat to social order—were all lies. Those who had him crucified are the guilty ones. God is innocent of all violence. The guilt lies entirely in envious, resentful, violent humanity.

The reason that "divinity goes into hiding" in the Passion is that the self-deception of violence can be demonstrated only when violence is given free rein, so that the murdered scapegoat later can be revealed as the Lamb of God.

Bergoglio points out that Christ's self-emptying silence—his meekness faced with the astonishing hostility mounted against him—is what causes the bad spirit to reveal itself, sure of its triumph. Jesus' defenselessness triggers an increase in the fury against him, for the weaker people are, the more ferociously they are attacked. "At the root of all ferocious attack is the need for people to project their own guilt and limitations," Bergoglio said in a retreat he gave in 1990. At such moments, he observes, the scapegoat mechanism comes into play, when "all the evils are offloaded onto the person we are ferociously attacking."

The effect of this "single victim mechanism" (as Girard calls it) is that everyone merges in hatred of the scapegoat. A perverse kind of unity—not a true unity, for it is based on a shared hatred rather than love—prevails: Pilate and Herod, who had been enemies, that day became friends (Luke 23:12). Even those who know Jesus to be innocent (his disciples, Pilate) go along with what is happening. Caught up in the mechanism, people are either convinced of the rightness of the violence directed against Jesus, or they are too stunned to oppose it. Hence Jesus' prayer from the Cross that they be forgiven, "for they do not know what they are doing" (Luke 23:34).

It is precisely this mechanism that will be revealed by the Resurrection, after which it can no longer be said that people do not know what they are doing. The self-deception of violent power, which reaches for justification by offloading guilt onto the poor and weak, can no longer be sustained. "In revealing the self-deception of those who engage in violence," writes Girard, "the New Testament dispels the lie at the heart of their violence."

So it is that, at the point when Jesus is defenseless and alone, the devil appears, triumphant, confident, convinced of victory. Bergoglio cites a seventh-century church father, Maximus the Confessor, who compares Christ on the Cross to the poisoned bait used by a fisherman. The flesh of Christ, writes Bergoglio, is "a baited hook," and the devil, in his fury and certainty of triumph—"this is your hour," says Jesus, "and the power of darkness" (Luke 22:53)—takes the bait, and poisons himself. The deception is unmasked. Evil remains, but it is no longer disguised as good; the camouflage no longer works. When Christ sees Satan "fall from heaven like a flash of lightning" (Luke 10:18), he is not announcing the end of Satan's existence but the end of his power to create order through false accusations that justify violence.

All of this, of course, is to come. The Resurrection will be the sign of a power breaking in from outside human experience and possibility, a power that transcends the world and allows us to see the truth. That power is the Spirit of God.

It is the Spirit that will reveal to Peter and later to Paul what they could not see when they were caught up in the contagious unanimity of the persecuting crowd.

It is the Spirit that allows the disciples—a small band, lacking in numbers and prestige, broken by what they have been through—to emerge to tell the truth of what happened on Calvary: humanity crucified the God who is all love.

It is the Spirit that gives the apostles the fortitude and the clarity to record that truth and live by what it reveals: the poor and wretched and despised of this earth are not the rejected of God but his beloved.

POINT FOR REFLECTION

What does it mean to say that Satan's power has been "unmasked"?

Little Brother

When I met with Pope Francis in May 2023, he gifted me with a short book titled *Il Fratellino*, which is a translation into Italian of what had been published first in Basque and in Spanish. In English, it is known as *Little Brother: An Odyssey to Europe*. He had mentioned the book several times in the previous months, recommended it to journalists on his flights, and had given copies to bishops and other visitors.

The story (mentioned earlier, in Day Five) of Ibrahima Balde's three-year journey across North Africa in search of his brother, Francis told the Jesuits in Malta, "makes us understand what it's like to cross the desert, as well as the traffic in migrants, the prisons, the tortures, the sea crossing." It is the migrants' way of the cross, revealing the human spirit and capacity for charity in the midst of cruelty and indifference to the fate of the poor.

Ibrahima's story begins in a poor village in Guinea in West Africa, from where he sets out across the deserts to Libya and Algeria. In Libya he learns that Alhassane and 143 other migrants lost their lives in a capsized Zodiac inflatable while attempting to reach Europe. Ibrahima ends up completing his brother's journey, making his way to Spain, where he now lives and works as a mechanic.

In buses, trucks, and on foot, doing jobs on building sites to make money for the next stage of the journey, Ibrahima contends not just with hostile terrain and alien cultures but also with abuse meted out to him at every stage. He is robbed, captured, imprisoned by slave-traders, tortured, shot at, chased away, beaten by police, forced to sleep on the street, and threatened with being shot by human traffickers if he refuses to board the boat. He undergoes every kind of physical and spiritual suffering, including the torment of guilt at being unable to save his brother.

Yet he also meets amazing kindness in angels who appear from nowhere. Ismail, a young boy, massages his legs swollen from weeks of walking in the desert. Emi, a Moroccan in Libya, helps him come to terms with his brother's death, and finds him work to give him hope for the next stage of the journey. After he makes it to Europe, he becomes friends with a Basque poet, Amets Arzallus Antia, at a homeless shelter center. Antia's spare, intense, vivid prose allows Ibrahima—who cannot read or write—to tell his story, which is a trial of suffering recounted without an ounce of self-pity.

There is a pattern here. From those in authority and who have power over him, Ibrahima usually meets contempt and abuse, while compassion and assistance nearly always come from people in similar conditions of precarity and vulnerability. It is as if there are two spirits at work in the human race.

Jesus, captive and alone, poor and powerless, his divinity invisible, triggers the same reactions. He is betrayed, captured, condemned, denied, interrogated, mocked, and tortured by those with power over him. But there are also those who dare to care: Simon who carries his cross; the centurion who recognizes his divinity; the women, including his mother, together with the "beloved disciple" in John's telling, at the foot of the cross. And there is Joseph of Arimathea, who lays him in a tomb.

By placing before us the truth about our human condition and the contrary spirits acting with us, the cross puts us in a crisis in the sense of the original Greek, *krisis*, meaning a choice or decision. On Calvary—and in the many, many Calvaries of our time—we are always given a choice: mercy, or sacrifice (Hosea 6:6). Sacrifice makes of the other an object, a means, something or someone that can be expended or disregarded to protect some interest or other. Mercy is to recognize the other's dignity and the need, and to respond by making room for them.

Sacrifice is what the religious people perform when they pass by the wounded man in the parable of the Good Samaritan. It is the indifference shown by Cain toward Abel in Genesis 4:9 ("Am I my brother's keeper?"). Mercy, on the other hand, is to choose to act, like the Samaritan, in response to the Spirit of God moving within him: "I have observed the misery of my people. . . . I have heard their cry . . . and I have come down to deliver them" (Exodus 3:7–8). It is to reach out, sense need, respond concretely, and create belonging. When we respond with mercy toward someone in need, we make real the truth that we belong to God and to one another. When we sacrifice the one in need, we deny that truth.

Francis is the greatest voice on the world stage telling the truth about the human condition: we belong to one another. His early *cri de coeur* from the island of Lampedusa in July 2013 still rings in the ears of the Western world, when he labeled the drowning of thousands of migrants "the globalization of indifference" and blasted a "culture of comfort, which makes us think only of ourselves." "Has anyone wept?" he asked in Lampedusa, before calling out "all those who in anonymity make social and economic decisions which open the door to tragic situations like this."

Since then he has consistently and constantly reminded us of the hundreds of thousands sacrificed in the borderlands of our world, those who are languishing in makeshift camps, or who ended up as bloated corpses on the beaches of the Mediterranean. As Western governments compete with one another to strengthen their borders, they force migrants into the hands of human traffickers who take increasingly more circuitous and dangerous routes across the seas. The justifications—that treating migrants humanely will "encourage more to come"—are those used since time immemorial to keep the poor from troubling those who are more fortunate. Thus does the rich world repel those it does not, will not, value.

In the United States, as this book was being written, alarming stories were emerging from Texas of hungry, exhausted migrants being pushed back into the Rio Grande by National Guardsmen and state troopers. There were accounts of drownings and broken limbs and miscarriages, and of children and pregnant mothers caught in huge bundles of razor wire. The pope's newspaper, *L'Osservatore Romano*, carried a picture above the headline "This Inhuman Wire." Archbishop Gustavo García-Siller of San Antonio, Texas, called it a "barbaric practice." Yet the four-billion-dollar Operation Lone Star by the state's governor, Greg Abbott, to deter "illegal immigration," was proving popular with many voters, for whom these sacrifices of human life were justified as a necessary deterrence.

Migration is a complex challenge with no simple solutions. But Francis is clear where policies must start. "This crisis which can be measured in numbers and statistics, we want instead to measure with names, stories, families," he said in 2016 at a Mass in the Mexican border town of Ciudad Juárez. He has insisted on this point over and over. Migration is not simply a problem. Migrants are people. And the Cross demands they be treated with compassion and dignity, as gifts to be received, not a burden to be shed or problem to be solved.

Jesus was treated not as a divinely created human being with a face and a story but as a problem to be solved by remote, anonymous powers. His life hung in the hands of people with no interest in him. The authorities who determined his fate did not know him and would not grieve for him. Those with the authority to investigate and judge his case chose not to use their power and influence to save him, because his death served their interests.

Matthew records that when morning came, "all the chief priests and the elders of the people conferred together against Jesus" (Matthew 27:1). His death was the main business on that day's agenda, the agreed-upon solution to a problem that was defined as a threat to the order and peace of the Jewish community and Roman rule.

So are today's migrants treated—as a threat to prosperity, as a problem for the host community to "solve," as a security risk. The logic of sacrifice is given free rein on Golgotha, as it is in the asylum and immigration systems of our world. The same mechanism that condemned Jesus operates now, in our time, and from within the heart of societies that claim to be Christian.

Addressing migrants in South Sudan, Francis noted how "great numbers of children born in recent years have known only the reality of camps for displaced persons," where, lacking memory of a home, losing all connection with their native land as well as their roots and their traditions, they live ghostly lives, unable to move forward or backward. He said, "The future cannot lie in refugee camps."

On Lesbos in Greece, he spoke of the stranding and capsizing of boats of refugees as a "shipwreck of civilization." He uses "bankruptcy of humanity" and "disgrace" to describe what he has seen. "We read stories of the concentration camps of the last century," he said in Cyprus, "and we say, 'How could this possibly have happened?' Brothers and sisters, it is happening today, on nearby coasts!"

The system of self-deceptive violence behind migration policies stands exposed and indicted in the shadow of Golgotha. Migration is not a security threat. In welcoming, protecting, promoting, and integrating migrants, we build civilizations of fraternity. In our capacity for welcoming the stranger as Christ, we become a "people" capable of acting "more and more as a single family dwelling in a common home," as Francis puts it in *Fratelli Tutti*.

Faced with the migration crisis, the Church led by Francis and his predecessors has seen in the stranger the wounds of Christ. In *Evangelii Gaudium* Francis calls countries to a "generous openness" that will create new, rich forms of diversity (EG 201–211); in *Laudato Si'* he highlights the tragic rise in migrants fleeing environmental degradation (LS 25); in *Amoris Laetitia* he speaks of the impact of migration on families (AL 46); in *Gaudete et Exsultate* he is astonished that any Christian could consider migration a secondary issue, and cites Scripture to make clear his concern is "not a notion invented by some pope" (GE 103). He has asked every parish and religious community to house at least one migrant family fleeing war or hunger. He has twice gone to the refugee camp on the Greek island of Lesbos and brought back refugees on the plane. And he has told religious communities facing decline to open the doors to refugees, telling them that "empty convents do not belong to you, they are for the flesh of Christ, which is what refugees are."

On the tenth anniversary of Lampedusa, Francis recalled the continued tragedies in the Mediterranean, where more than twenty-seven thousand have died since 2014. In his letter he spoke of "the silent massacres before which we still remain helpless and stunned." And he restated Jesus' message in Matthew 25, that "the brother who knocks at the door deserves love, hospitality and every care," because "he is a brother who, like me, has been placed on earth to enjoy what exists there and to share it in communion." He added, "The Church is called to come out of herself, soothing with the balm of fraternity and charity the bleeding sores of those who bear the same wounds of Christ imprinted on their own bodies."

POINT FOR REFLECTION

How do you understand the idea that migrants and refugees are the "flesh of Christ"?

Assuming Failure

In two retreats Bergoglio gave in 1990 to priests in La Plata, Argentina, he drew on a theology book that had been helpful to him at the time. Bergoglio read *Triumph through Failure* in its Italian translation, *Teologia del Fallimento* ("A Theology of Failure").

"The Cross raised the question of failure which the Resurrection answered," wrote the author, American Jesuit John J. Navone. On those days leading up to the Crucifixion, and on Golgotha itself, God seemed to have failed Jesus. Yet in reality that failure began much earlier—from the sixth chapter of John's Gospel, after Jesus began speaking of his body and blood as food and drink. From that time on, as in the synoptic Gospels, a sense of gloom and foreboding spreads through the narrative. Misunderstandings sprout. Opposition builds. From chapter eight, Jesus is in almost permanent conflict with hostile groups. It is clear by now that his mission to convert Israel has failed by a country mile. He has let down his disciples, who had believed he would be successful, and he has disappointed all who had hoped for freedom from Roman rule.

For all the healing and hope Jesus had brought to perhaps thousands of people, there was no sign by this time that he had transformed the culture, powers, and societal structures of his time. After he died, abandoned by all but a few disciples, there was no sign of the Church he had asked Peter to lead, the Church that would continue his mission. When Jesus let out his last gasp, all that was left was a group of shattered, fearful, confused followers muttering, "We had hoped" (Luke 24:21).

To enter into the Passion is to imagine ourselves as part of that failure. It is to picture ourselves in Jerusalem, fleeing Golgotha, and trying to explain to a visitor who Jesus was. The visitor would see only another distastefully brutal punishment of some provincial wretch on the forgotten edges of an empire, with the connivance of corrupt local religious leaders. Would I be able to explain otherwise? "We had hoped," the disciples say after Jesus' death. Was it all a dream? Did we ever really believe this? When Ignatius asks us to contemplate divinity going into hiding, we must not turn our eyes from the depth of the human failure Jesus took on. Faced with the prospect of the Passion, he is overpowered, three times praying to be spared what is to come. As Karl Rahner writes, "The Father does not budge. . . . The request for the passing of the chalice is drowned in silence." But by the third prayer, Jesus has accepted what is to come, and has new energy and decisiveness: "Get up, let us be going" (Mark 14:42). His submission allows him to receive the grace he needs.

Because of his acceptance, Jesus is never weighed down or deterred by *fear* of failure. His suffering is intense and relentless. Yet even when he feels the absence of the Father to whom he has dedicated all, Jesus never loses his trust that God will act, somehow, to save humanity. Jesus trusts that it will be precisely through this failure, in the place of the catastrophe, that God will create the new thing, will open the new horizon. Jesus is completely attuned to the logic of the divine plan of salvation in which there is an "inexorable link between the willing and courageous acceptance of complete failure in one's historical life-story, and the successful accomplishment of the divine will," as Navone puts it.

That divine will is recognized only later, in retrospect, only after that historical life story is over. God will begin to act while the world sleeps, when the tomb is dark and empty and silent and the corpse is still, and all hope has died.

In his La Plata retreats Bergoglio described this embrace of failure as Jesus "entering into patience." Jesus endures, is constant, holds fast, awaits. His failure in worldly terms is total, yet he succeeds in the one thing that matters: the fulfilment of God's will. He defeats sin by radical hope in God's action. As St. Mother Teresa of Kolkata, who lived long dark nights of spiritual aridity, once put it, "God has not called me to be successful; He has called me to be faithful."

To take up our cross is to hear that call. It is to trust that God will act, often beyond the point where, humanly speaking, all solutions have failed. For Jesus, what mattered was not just to endure—this was not a stoic act—but to do so in obedience to God's will and in confidence in God's action. No level of pain and heartbreak, including his own visceral sense of abandonment by God, ever reduced his utter confidence in God's power and loving action.

Bergoglio reminded the Jesuits that this is the element that every Christian is called to embrace if they are to live by the gospel:

It is precisely on the Cross that Jesus definitively assumes failure and evil, and transcends them. It is there that he shows the unfathomable depths of his love, for only one who loves much has the freedom and the spiritual vitality to accept failure. Jesus dies a failure ... and in his death he assumes and brings to fulfilment all the failures of salvation history. Now there remains but one solution: the divine solution, in this case the Resurrection as the ferment of a revolution.

This means that the Christian has to incorporate into his or her daily life the conviction that Jesus Christ is among us. Otherwise their Christianity is a pseudo-failure: by avoiding the scandalous failure of the Cross which is the total annihilation of human hope, by not "hoping against all hope," their lives will be no more than a series of twists and turns through a more acceptable failure of the prettily packaged variety, a failure that can elegantly co-exist with universal, everyman values, the failure of a religion without true belief, because it lacks the anointing of all true belief: Jesus Christ, risen, alive among us.

This is a profound insight we can spend a lifetime absorbing. The "freedom and spiritual vitality" of the one who loves much comes from her lack of fear of failure. That fear turns people anxiously in on themselves, condemning them to the "pseudo-failure" of mediocrity, what Bergoglio calls the "more acceptable failure of the pretty packaged variety." Put differently, the kind of failure that does not turn us in on ourselves in disappointment but opens us to God's saving action is not ultimately a failure at all but the opposite: a seedbed of possibility, in which God will sow the future.

Failure in our lives, Navone says, is very often the way God delivers us from the illusion of our self-sufficiency, the danger of "believing more in ourselves than in God." Failure that rescues us from self-sufficiency makes space for God's resurrecting action. "The beginning of faith is to know that we need salvation," as Francis put it in his famous message from St. Peter's Square the night of March 27,

2020, when half of the world was in COVID lockdown. "We are not self-sufficient; alone, we drown."

When Jesus washed the feet of the disciples prior to his trial and Crucifixion, writes Navone, he showed that it is "fraternal love, rather than historic success or failure, that counts before God." Jesus teaches by his act that there is no self-transcendence, no fraternal love, without willingness to endure the pain of failure in the expectation of God's action. The road to love and freedom of spirit begins in the willingness to share in the ultimate self-transcendence of the Crucifixion.

What the Cross also teaches us is that for God, weakness and failure are the places where he acts. Our limitations and wounds become the open places God can enter. The constraints we face in our lives and mission—the limitations of others, the scarcity of resources, our own painful shortcomings—are not a reason to chafe and complain but the place of our prayerful hope. The only true failure, then, is not to see that hope, to remain convinced that all depends on us. As Portuguese cardinal José Tolentino Mendonça told Pope Francis and the Curia at their 2018 retreat,

> The great obstacle to the life of God within us is not frailty or weakness, but hardness and rigidity. It is not vulnerability and humiliation, but their opposite: pride, self-sufficiency, self-justification, isolation, violence, the delirium of power. . . . The strength of what we really need, the grace that is so necessary to us, is not ours but Christ's. And it is he who gives us the example of embracing humanity entirely in all its drama, since it was "in his wounds we were healed" (Isa 53:5).

To "enter into patience"—from the Latin *patientia*, meaning suffering—is to live as Jesus did: to belong first to God, obeying his will, working humbly, within the limits of ordinary daily life. It means to accept and not turn away from wounds that life and others have inflicted upon us, as well as those that we have inflicted on others.

When he has risen, Jesus will be known by his wounds. Seeing and touching them is how his disciples will verify that he is the same one who suffered those wounds on their behalf. When our wounds become the door through which God's mercy pours into the world, we can begin to live truthfully, not denying our human condition.

Ecce homo, declares Pilate, when Jesus is brought out, bruised and broken. *Here is the human.* The Roman governor who asked, "Truth? What is that?" has spoken the truth. Francis insists on this: There is no other way of sharing Christ's mission and receiving God's mercy than by following the wounds of Jesus to the wounds of our own world.

In Washington, D.C., in September 2015, Francis said, "The price of lasting victory is allowing ourselves to be wounded and consumed." For when we look upon his wounds and do not turn away, we are led to where Christ is and to where humanity is. We move out beyond ourselves, unarmed and vulnerable, and into direct contact with the suffering of the world. There we will meet the wounds of Christ, and they will be the wounds on his risen body.

POINT FOR REFLECTION

How ready am I to "enter into patience"?

SPIRITUAL EXERCISES, DAY 7 (WEEK 3)

Contemplation of the Passion (SE 190–203)

- *Read:* Jesus' foretelling of his Passion in Mark 8:31–33, Mark 9:31–32, and Mark 10:32–34. Imagine that you are among the disciples listening to him. How do they react, and why? How do *you* react?
- *Read:* The Passion of our Lord Jesus Christ (in any of the four Gospels), considering Jesus' sufferings "for my sins, and what I ought to do and suffer for him" (SE 195, 197). Consider how "the divinity hides itself" (SE 196) and how the created world takes part in the Passion.
- *Grace to ask for:* "Sorrow, compassion and shame because the Lord is going to His suffering for my sins" (SE 193), and to experience "sorrow with Christ in sorrow, anguish with Christ in anguish, tears and deep grief because of the great anguish Christ endures for me" (SE 203).

Contemplate-Discern-Propose

- *Contemplate:* Any contemporary situation of suffering (e.g., migration) with which you are familiar, locally or nationally or globally.
- *Discern:* What would it mean to "enter into patience" and to "touch the flesh of Christ" in this circumstance? What is revealed and unmasked?
- *Propose:* How could you respond and act?

See Jesus as happy, overflowing with joy. Rejoice with him as with a friend who has triumphed. They killed him, the holy one, the just one, the innocent one, but he triumphed in the end. Evil does not have the last word. Nor will it have the last word in your life, for you have a friend who loves you and wants to triumph in you.

Your Saviour lives.

—Pope Francis

DAY EIGHT

A New Imagination of the Possible

*On Sharing Christ's Joy and His Peace
in the Galilee of Today*

The Consoler

The shift is dramatic. As we enter the fourth week, Ignatius asks us now to consider "the divinity, which seemed to hide itself during the Passion, now appearing and manifesting itself so miraculously in the most holy Resurrection in its true and most sacred effects" (SE 223). After our compassion with Jesus in his suffering, now is the hour of rejoicing in his resurrected life. We promised to be with him in his agony; now we follow him into his glory, deepening and confirming that promise in the concrete mission of our lives.

As in his Crucifixion, so in his Resurrection: we are invited to contemplate Christ, to touch his wounds, to join ourselves to him, to love as he loves. The risen Christ's greeting to us, his followers—"Peace be with you"—is the news of the triumph of the Cross. This peace is what Ignatius calls consolation. It is "when an interior movement is aroused in the soul, by which it is inflamed with love of its Creator and Lord," as well as "every increase of faith, hope and love, and all interior joy that invites and attracts to what is heavenly," by filling our hearts with "peace and quiet in its Creator and Lord" (SE 316).

Ignatius asks us to contemplate "the office of consoler that Christ our Lord exercises" (SE 224) and to take on that same mission.

This peace is not the peace of tranquility or indifference; it is not the peace the world gives (John 14:27). The peace the risen Lord brings is the overflowing joy of knowing that we belong. We are loved and can love. We are in good hands. We can trust in life. It is the peace that allows us to seek the will of God, to go out on mission and bring Christ's healing consolation to others. It is peace with oneself, knowing freedom from inflexibility, anger, and impatience. It is also the kind of peace that allows us to encounter others not as rivals but as gifts. And it is peace with creation, learning to live in partnership with all that is created and is good.

It is also the peace that comes suddenly and unexpectedly, when God acts through "overflow," breaking into a dead-end of conflict with the promise of new life and possibility. It is when we open ourselves to "a new imagination of the possible with the realism that only the Gospel can give us," as Francis put it in a COVID pandemic meditation. By realism, Francis meant that the Resurrection is neither an abstract concept nor a spectacular one-off event but a concrete experience of God's action in daily life. Its "sacred effects" are in us, both as individuals and as his people; they bring us out of ourselves, lead us outward in mission, allow us to take part in history, opening up this era to be reshaped by the kingdom of God.

It is the peace of a new way forward, the peace of breakthroughs that surpass our understanding. It is the peace that opens a new dawn of clarity and harmony where before there was division and darkness. It is the peace of forgiveness that comes to a relationship headed for breakup. It is the peace that comes to a lost and restless person who at last finds their calling. It is the peace opened by an unexpected end to a time of suffering. It is the peace brought by the healing of past wounds that, even if the scars are still visible, now lose their grip on us and free us for a deeper loving.

It is the peace that comes from facing a difficult truth about ourselves and being freed for growth. It is the amazing peace of deep insight, such as Ignatius had by the river Cardoner, when he was given a total sense of how all creatures emanate from God and through Christ return to God, and how each creature contributes to God's plan. It is the peace of awe that comes on us when we see a bird circling in the sky, or smell a flower flaunting its fragrance, or when we feel the divine energy coursing through all creation. It is the peace that happens every time God resurrects some part of us, when we have opened ourselves to the action of his grace and have not blocked it by turning in on ourselves. Such moments are a source of joy *for us*; but these are also moments of joy *with Christ* (SE 48).

And yet outwardly, the world carries on as before. The resurrections in our lives are often hard to explain or put into words. Our cups overflow off-radar, in concealed, intimate ways. Perhaps only a few people close to us can even see what has taken place; even we may struggle to describe it. Even so, we know by its signs that a transfiguration has occurred. Unearned, as if from the outside, the peace has come upon us, and it is life defining, if not life changing. To those who have experienced it, nothing will ever be the same, and they want to sing it from the rooftops—even if down there the river of life is flowing through the streets as if this is just another day.

What happened on the Sunday of the Resurrection and in the weeks that followed was like that. From the angels in the empty tomb to the beach breakfast in Galilee, the risen Jesus came to console his followers in a strange in-between world of sadness and hope, disappointment and elation, broken dreams and limitless horizons. Jesus is here with them, yet now, just as suddenly, he is not. He eats with them, shows his wounds, touches and is touched, and yet he dissolves and reappears through locked doors. It *is* he, but he is a Jesus so altered that Mary Magdalene recognizes him only when he says her name (John 20:11–18). The disciples on the road to Emmaus know him only when he gives the blessing over the bread after a day's walk with them (Luke 24:13–35).

For all their joy, the disciples are hesitant; the community gradually begins to piece together what has happened and what it all means. Francis described this time in a Pentecost homily as "fifty days of uncertainty." Referring to John's Gospel (John 20:19–26), he says, "True, Jesus had risen. Overjoyed, they had seen him, listened to his words and even shared a meal with him. Yet they had not overcome their doubts and fears: they met behind closed doors."

Only after Jesus' ascension and the coming of the Spirit at Pentecost will the apostles achieve an intimacy with Christ even greater than they had while he was with them on earth. This is the new life that Jesus pledged would come when he promised to ask the Father to send his Spirit to abide with his followers (John 14:17). In this way, he told them at the Last Supper, they would know "that I am in my Father, and you in me, and I in you" (John 14:20). This is a new belonging brought about by the Resurrection and then, completely, at Pentecost. It has been available ever since to all believers. It is the belonging that leads St. Paul to tell the Romans, "The Spirit of God dwells in you. Anyone who does not have the Spirit of Christ does not belong to him" (Romans 8:9).

Ignatius invites us to ask for the grace "to be glad and rejoice intensely because of the great joy and the glory of Christ our Lord" (SE 221). We should ask for this grace of joy, says Francis, not for our own sake, but "out of love for the message, since joy is constitutive of the Gospel." Joy is apostolic. It is "a clear indicator of grace," he told the meeting of Jesuits in Rome, adding: "It indicates that love is active, operative, present." Even in their titles, Francis's teaching documents—*The Joy of the Gospel, The Joy of Love, Rejoice and Be Glad*—point to joy as the mark of life in God.

An Argentine Jesuit who knew Bergoglio well, Fr. Juan Carlos Scannone, SJ, once told me that one of Francis's great spiritual gifts was his capacity to "rejoice in the joy of the people"—the gift, he said, of the Fourth Week. When Francis goes around St. Peter's Square greeting pilgrims, hugging the elderly, and blessing babies, he is not just radiating joy but resonating with the joy of those who have come out to be with him. Francis is energized and uplifted—rejuvenated—by the joy of Christ in his people.

Joy did not come easily to the disciples at first, turned inward as they were in desolation, fear, and self-focus. Nor does it come naturally to most of us. Perhaps there is a "stone of distrust" that keeps us entombed, or some deep-seated fear (of failure, or disillusionment) that has us looking down at the ground (Luke 24:5). At the 2019 Easter Vigil, Francis asked us to name that stone, and to ask the risen Lord to roll it away so that we can catch sight of the new horizon of possibility. Can we enter that joy, can we rejoice with Christ risen? What keeps us back, holds us in? What grace must we ask for?

One way into that joy is through Mary of Magdala when Jesus speaks her name in the quiet stillness of the garden at dawn, outside the empty tomb (John 20:11–18). Because Mary was the first to bear witness to the risen Christ, Francis in 2016 elevated her celebration in the liturgical calendar to a feast day, honoring her as the "apostle to the apostles."

Francis often highlights the point that the women disciples in Matthew (28:1–10), Mark (16:1–8), and Luke (24:1–11) were the first to grasp what had happened. The reason why is important. Like all the disciples, their sorrow was mixed with the cold dread of being surrounded by a hostile city. But the women "knew how to just be and to accompany others," says Francis in the COVID meditation.

They were not paralyzed, as the male apostles were; even in their desolation they could still give of themselves in practical action. They continued to trust. Because they loaded their bags with spices and went off at first light to anoint Jesus' body, they were the first to see the stone rolled away and to peer inside the empty tomb, and hear the angels tell them that Jesus was no longer there, among the dead. Their fear and loss turned to a joy that has them, in Matthew and Luke, running to the others to tell them what they had seen, bearing the message that Jesus was "going ahead of you to Galilee; there you will see him" (Matthew 28:7).

> ## POINT FOR REFLECTION
>
> Who am I in this? One of those carrying the spices at dawn, or one of those staying behind closed doors?

Galilee

The paralysis of the disciples was understandable. They had lost not just the one they loved but the dream they had given their lives to. "We had hoped," the disciples tell the stranger on the way to Emmaus (Luke 24:21). It is easy to imagine them as divided and disoriented. Perhaps some were determined to continue Jesus' mission against hopeless odds, while others wanted to take the path of beleaguered resistance. Perhaps others said it was better to give up and go home. What was the point now, when the dream had turned to dust?

What changed everything was the empty tomb and the message: Jesus was going ahead of them to Galilee, where they would see him, as he had promised (Mark 16:7; Matthew 28:7). In his Easter Vigil homilies since 2020, Francis has returned constantly to this commission by the risen Christ, because of its relevance to our own time.

Galilee was the area furthest from the ritual purity of the holy city; it was a place of the gentiles, an outpost on the periphery where people of different religions lived, and a place of poverty. Galilee also means daily life, the ordinary streets we travel, the place we knew before but now must go to again, the place of our new mission. Going to Galilee means to come out of hiding and shelter and to meet Jesus again, but in a new way. We know the place, but we see it as if for the first time in the company of the risen Christ. We are being sent to Galilee to learn to live in the gap between the scarcity of our means and the enormity of God's mission, to learn to depend not on our own power, but on God's. Jesus "goes before us" to enable that mission.

Francis places such emphasis on this going to Galilee because he is convinced the Church today is called to do the same. Just as, as far as the world is concerned, what happened on Golgotha might be the death of another person of no importance, so today the former Christian cultures of the West treat the Cross as a fable. Just as, then, the only ones who know differently are few in number and of little social standing, so today Christians have become a disregarded minority. As Francis told the Roman Curia in 2019: "Brothers and sisters, Christendom no longer exists! Today we are no longer the ones who create culture, nor are we in the forefront of those most listened to."

Secularization means the Western Church can no longer start out from the center of the city, where cathedrals stand alone in a sea of offices and shopping malls. There is a freedom and a grace here, in the poverty of our means. The Church must again start from Galilee, which is to say from the margins, from places of longing and need. The margins for the Church are the new horizon of possibility, the place from where, amazingly, the Church of the future will gradually be reborn and grow.

There has long been a shift within the Catholic Church worldwide, away from the white, wealthy centers, where it is atrophying, to the poorer and more peripheral areas of the world, where it is growing fast. But where the Church is dying, it is doing so not because of its decline in numbers but because of its failure in practice to believe in the promise of the Resurrection, which is "secretly woven into the fabric of this history" (EG 278). The Church will fail in the West only if it surrenders to the temptations in times of desolation: in nostalgia for the past, or sterile debates about ideas, refusing to be converted to a new way of being. The synod process is designed by Francis to counter this temptation, to send the Church to Galilee, where Jesus is waiting.

A writer who understands this call of Francis is the Czech priest-philosopher Tomáš Halík. He takes Francis's oft-used phrase, that this is not an era of change but a change of era, and names the transition Francis refers to, using the metaphors of the stages of the day. We have moved, Fr. Halík says, from early morning (the early Church) and the later morning (Christendom) through the long mid-day of modernity. Now we are in the noontime eclipse of that era, a time of transition to the new epoch of the "afternoon" of Christianity. In this transition, made possible in the Church by synodality, there is a renewed call to recover something of the early morning. From a place of humility and powerlessness, the church is called to a Galilee-style mission, not to proselytize or reconquest but to evangelize by listening deeply and serving the margins.

Just as Jesus' risen form was not immediately recognized but he was known by his voice, his wounds, and his breaking of bread, so the Church will take on new forms that at first will seem different. The Church of the Byzantine era looked very strange compared to the Church of Jerusalem, and the Church of modernity would be in many respects unrecognizable to the medieval Church. So, too, the Church of the afternoon will look different from the Church of midday.

"The process of secularization has not caused the disappearance of Christianity, as some expected, but its transformation," Fr. Halík told the European synodal assembly in Prague in March 2023. That transformation means recovering elements lost or neglected in the long centuries of Christendom, not least of which is the turn toward synodality, to a Church in which all the baptized learn to walk together and participate in a deep listening to where the Spirit is trying to guide us.

In *The Afternoon of Christianity,* Fr. Halík takes Francis's core call and puts it thus: "The time is come," he says, "for the self-transcendence of Christianity." It is called to transcend existing mental, institutional, confessional, cultural, and other boundaries in order to fulfill its universal mission. It will be a challenge to discern what that transcendence will entail, to distinguish between what, outside the boundaries, is a gift of God the Church is called to receive, and what is a distraction. That is why discernment is key.

Self-transcendence is perhaps *the* great theme of the Francis pontificate: a Church that comes out of itself in service of all. It is a Church that honors the diversity and freedom of others, renouncing all proselytism and desire for control, trusting in God's power and taking seriously the guidance of the Holy Spirit. It is a Church called now to resist all the temptations of the closed doors of the Upper Room, all the egocentric temptations of clericalism, fundamentalism, traditionalism, and triumphalism that in *Evangelii Gaudium* Francis calls "the bitter poison of immanence" (EG 87).

As Francis told the Curia in 2019, rigidity, born of the fear of change, is the great temptation that faces the Church, just as it was for the disciples in the Upper Room. Acting as if all depended on them alone, they erected fences and drew up the drawbridge in an effort to feel secure.

"If amidst all the historic transformations our faith must remain a Christian faith, now the mark of its identity is the kenosis, the gift of self, self-renunciation, transcending oneself," says Father Halík. The Church of the future, he says, will be discovered not among the tombs of the past but "in the Galilee of today," in the world of the seekers and the people of no religious affiliation. There, we will discover Jesus, says Halík, "surprisingly transformed" and known by his wounds, beyond the visible confines of the Church.

In calling us to Galilee, Jesus asks us to meet him in two places in particular: in the poor and in community. The first is the place of need, of thirst, of pain and longing. The second is the place where the people are gathered, which is the very Body that Jesus seeks to form. In part 3 of *Let Us Dream*, Francis invites us to the Galilee of our own time to help build the dignity of the people that Jesus comes to affirm. This is an invitation to enter into and walk with those who struggle on the peripheries in social movements, for "it was precisely here that the Church was born, in the shadow of the Cross where so many of the crucified are found."

Throughout history, noted Bergoglio in 1991, "the Church's true reforms, those that bring life to parts of it that are dead, are born from within the entrails of the Church itself." To go out to Galilee, to embrace Christ's consoling mission to the crucified, to listen deeply to those searching, is what will bring new life to the Church in our time. The new life will come from the faithful people on whom the Spirit has been poured, the people in the shadow of the Cross who know how to suffer in patience and rejoice with the risen Christ. It is they who depend on God to be set free from every form of enslavement. It is they to whom the Church must come out of itself to meet.

POINT FOR REFLECTION

How do I react to this idea of the Church in the process of a transition to a new era?

Contemplatio

Ignatius's "Contemplation to Attain the Love of God" (SE 230–237) helps us go out of ourselves and into a deeper belongingness with the Creator, creation, and our fellow creatures. *Attain* is something of a misnomer: the Spanish word Ignatius uses, *alcanzar*, is closer to "reach" or "arrive at." It is not a matter of our efforts but our receptivity. The call is to reach a place where we can "love more" because we know deep inside the gift that is God. It is to love as God loves.

"We think back not only on his revealed Word, but also on our own lives, the lives of others, and all that the Lord has done in his Church," says Francis in *Gaudete et Exsultate*. "God wished to enter history, and so our prayer is interwoven with memories. . . . This is the grateful memory that Saint Ignatius of Loyola refers to in his Contemplation for Attaining Love" (GE 153). The grace of this prayer is to *love more* through grasping with the heart that *all is gift*.

The first part of the contemplation is my memory of my own past as a person, but also the history of God's holy faithful people to whom I belong. "Think of your own history when you pray," says Francis, "and there you will find much mercy" (GE 153). From that history of mercy we move to the present and then to the future. The *contemplatio* asks us to look at creation and see God's life-giving power at work there, and to respond by knowing God as the source of all that is good.

Ignatius wants us to take note of two points. The first is that *love is known in actions rather than words* (SE 230). While words can deceive and be empty, actions are concrete; they speak for themselves. When we are bringing to mind and heart what God does for us, or what we can do for God, it is on acts that we need to focus. (But an act need not be solely in the realm of the physical. When we pledge ourselves to God's service, for example, this is an act.)

The second is that *love is always a mutual sharing*; it involves an exchange of gifts, such that "the lover gives and shares with the beloved what he possesses, or something of what he has or is able to give" (SE 231). This sharing is what we do in the *contemplatio*. Referring to chapter 26 of the book of Deuteronomy, Francis recalls in *Let Us Dream* (28) how Moses prescribed that after taking possession of the land, the Israelites were to recall the history of their people in a prayer of gratitude. The prayer began, "A wandering Aramean was my ancestor." That prayer, Francis notes, "is a story of shame and redemption," of being sold into slavery, calling on the Lord's name, and being brought out of Egypt to their own land. "The ignominy of our past, in other words, is part of what and who we are."

Ignatius places us before God and his angels and saints (SE 232) to ask for the grace of "an intimate knowledge of the many blessings received, that filled with gratitude for all, we may in all things love and serve the Divine Majesty" (233). He then suggests some points for our reflection.

The first is to "recall to mind the blessings of creation and redemption, and the special favors I have received" (SE 234). This is a chance to retread the tracks of God's graces in my life, perhaps over a particular time, or even in this past week of the retreat, using Deuteronomy 8:2–6, as Bergoglio suggests in one of his retreat talks. The idea is to recall the blessings or gifts in three areas.

1. **The blessings of creation** are those of the natural world but also of the world I have helped to create (family, community, profession) and which have been the place of my generativity and creativity.

2. **The blessings of redemption** are all the examples of healing, forgiveness, and new life I have experienced, often through particular people (teachers, pastors, mentors, and guides) who have helped me bridge rough waters and enter into new pastures. Among these gifts are sins or failures which, like the jars of dirty water used for absolutions that Jesus at Cana turns into fine wine (John 2:1–12), God's grace has turned into sources of life.

3. **The special favors or specific blessings** are what the Church calls skills, or passions (leading, teaching, healing, preaching, envisioning) that are or could be used for building up the Church. These last are particularly important for the Church of the future, which needs to better honor and deploy the charisms that the Spirit is pouring out on his people. But first it is for *us* to recognize and honor these gifts.

After the first point, Ignatius invites us to make the *Suscipe,* which is an "offering of myself," in his famous prayer:

Take, Lord, and receive all my liberty, my memory, my understanding, and my entire will, all that I have and possess. Thou hast given all to me. To Thee, O Lord, I return it. All is Thine, dispose of it wholly according to Thy will. Give me Thy love and Thy grace, for this is sufficient for me. (SE 234)

The next three points (SE 235–237) ask us to turn to creation, to see how "God dwells in creatures," giving them life and sensation, and does the same for his human creatures, to whom he also gives the capacity to understand and know (SE 235). Ignatius asks us to consider how God "works and labors for me in all creatures upon the face of the earth" (SE 236), giving life and being to all that exists, which is the source of what we need to thrive: food, water, sustainable climate, and good health. Finally he invites us to "consider all blessings and gifts as descending from above," including my own "limited power" as well as "justice, mercy, goodness, etc." All these, says Ignatius, "descend from above as the rays of light descend from the sun, and as the waters flow from their fountains" (SE 137).

These are powerful, joyful invitations to go to the source of our being and of all life, and to stand in the waterfall with arms outstreched. For this part of the *contemplatio,* it is again good to go outside, to discover not just God's action in the soul but also his action—the *ruah,* his life-spirit—in all things. We can take with us, in our hands or hearts, the final fourteen paragraphs of *Laudato Si'* (LS 233–246), so that we might see how God inhabits his gift by filling the universe completely, from the greatest ocean down to the tiniest ant and atom.

What Ignatius asks us to see is God at work in the generative, growing power of living things. The sheer dynamic exuberance of creation—the urge to grow and flourish and propagate—also reveals the deep interconnectedness of all creatures in it. Each creature, says Saint Bonaventure (quoted in LS 240), bears the imprint of the Trinity, such that creatures tend toward God and other living things in "secretly interwoven relationships."

And the same is true of us, for the human person "grows more, matures more and is sanctified more to the extent that he or she enters into relationships, going out from themselves to live in communion with God, with others and with all creatures" (LS 240). To experience this we must not just *go out* but *go out of ourselves*—to see this interconnectedness, to see how other created things self-transcend in a dynamic exchange of gifts, and how this design is reflected in them. Can we perceive this design, and perceive it reflected in us as well?

Ignatius knew that we understand better how God lovingly acts in us when we see God at work in his creation. Because the whole world came out of God, we can love God only in and through his creation—loving him in all creatures, and loving all creatures in him. In this way we can catch God at work in his creation, loving it and us into flourishing, just as we can know the sun from its rays or the source of water in what flows from it (SE 237). Ignatius wrote to Francis Borgia in 1545 that "when people go out of themselves and enter in their Creator and Lord, they receive continuous instruction, attention and consolation, and come to see how our eternal good is found in all created things, giving them being and sustaining them with his infinite being and presence."

This is not so easy for us now, for "we no longer have the gaze of Saint Francis, who looked at the sun—which he called brother because so he felt it to be," notes Francis in his apostolic letter *Desiderio Desideravi* (DD 44). But now, emerging from the eclipse of modernity, entering the afternoon of Christianity, is a time to recover "confidence about creation," as Francis, in the same letter, explains: "If created things are such a fundamental, essential part of the sacramental action that brings about our salvation, then we must arrange ourselves in their presence with a fresh, non-superficial regard, respectful and grateful" (DD 46).

Let us put ourselves before creation in respect and gratitude, and contemplate the gifts that flow between God, his creation, and his creatures. And in the light of *Laudato Si'* and the ecological crisis that reflects our rupture with nature, we might conclude by offering ourselves both to God and to the care of his creation. We give of ourselves in response to his self-giving, not just in the silence of our hearts but also when we are at work in the fields and the gardens, making some humble offering of hospitality to nature.

To Go Out

"The Lord wants an evangelizing Church, I see that clearly," Francis told the Jesuits in Peru in 2018. "This came from my heart, in simplicity, in the few minutes I spoke during the general congregations before the conclave." As he had done in Aparecida six years earlier, Francis spoke of how the Holy Spirit calls us out of ourselves, inviting us to abandon all the worldliness and self-sufficiency that prevents us from responding to that invitation. The Holy Spirit, Francis said in his first Pentecost homily, "draws us into the mystery of the living God and saves us from the threat of a Church which is gnostic and self-referential, closed in on herself. He urges us to open the doors and go forth to proclaim and bear witness to the good news of the Gospel, to communicate the joy of faith, the encounter with Christ. The Holy Spirit is the soul of mission."

At the conclusion of this retreat, it would be good to revisit chapter 5 of *Evangelii Gaudium* to hear that call which Francis makes on behalf of Jesus Christ, and to combine it with the fourth—"ecclesial"—dream of *Querida Amazonia*. It is a call born of the desire expressed in the *Suscipe* prayer that we share the experience we have received in this week. For "what kind of love would not feel the need to speak of the beloved, to point him out, to make him known?" (EG 264). This is how Christianity first spread: through testimony by ordinary people. And it is how it will spread again, in the "afternoon" of Christianity. "All the baptized," says Francis, "whatever their position in the Church or their level of instruction in the faith, are agents of evangelization" (EG 120).

In the course of this retreat we have, hopefully, found the joy of the Lord, which he promised us would fill our hearts and not be taken from us (John 16:22). The news of God's infinite love for every man and woman "must constantly resound" in every place, says Francis (QA 64). It is a rejuvenating, reinvigorating love, healing and consoling and liberating all at the same time. It is made to be shared.

The way we are loved by God is beautifully expressed in chapter 4 of the 2018 exhortation *Christus Vivit*, which followed the synod on young people. Francis urges us to read it to grasp the message of God's infinite love for every man and woman (QA 64). It is not long, but it is very rich. And as we read it, slowly and contemplatively, we should let it affect us as we absorb the "three truths" it captures: that God loves me, that Christ is my Savior, and that he is alive.

How we communicate and proclaim that message will be different. It must take flesh in the time and place where every believer is sent as a missionary disciple, with a passion to serve not only Jesus but also his people. "He takes us from the midst of his people and he sends us to his people; without this sense of belonging we cannot understand our deepest identity" (EG 268). We are part of a people, called to be a people, and the church must be "open to the multiplicity of gifts that the Holy Spirit bestows on every one. For wherever there is a particular need, he has already poured out the charisms that can meet it" (QA 94).

Francis asks us to embrace this dual identity of belonging both to Jesus *and* to his people, and to accept this identity as the true source of our belonging. Because all of us are "a mission on this earth," Francis writes, "we have to regard ourselves as sealed, even branded, by this mission of bringing light, blessing, enlivening, raising up, healing and freeing" (EG 273). This mission is evangelization. It is to proclaim the dignity of a people raised up by God's closeness and offer them a horizon of hope. And if the people of God have a particular calling at this time, it is to do what Jesus did: "He came to strengthen and deepen the bonds of belonging—of the people to God and to each other. That is why the one who matters most in the Kingdom of God is whoever makes himself least, serving others, and especially the poor" (LUD 105).

Many believers are nervous about being asked to evangelize, associating it with a kind of apologetics that sets out to convince others, or a sort of marketing strategy. But in a catechesis on evangelization in January 2023, Francis described evangelizing this way:

> Our proclamation begins today, there where we live. And it does not begin by trying to convince others, not to convince: but by bearing witness every day to the beauty of the Love that has looked upon us and lifted us up. And it is this beauty, communicating this beauty, that will convince people—not communicating *ourselves* but *the Lord himself.* We proclaim *the Lord.* We do not proclaim ourselves, we do not proclaim a political party, an ideology. No: we proclaim Jesus. We need to put Jesus in contact with the people, without convincing them but allowing the Lord to do the convincing. . . . The Church grows not by proselytism, it grows by attraction.

What allows us to do this is the Spirit; the Spirit shows us how and gives us the means. A Church called out of itself to evangelize is one that depends not on its own strength but on that of the Spirit, which Jesus promised would come to his followers at Pentecost. The Spirit, he said, would be with them, and would lead them into the fullness of truth. "When Jesus says to His disciples—and also to us—'Go!,' he is not just communicating a word," Francis said in another catechesis. "No. He simultaneously communicates the Holy Spirit, because it is only thanks to Him, thanks to the Holy Spirit, that one can receive Christ's mission and carry it out (cf. John 20:21–22)."

The Holy Spirit decenters us and leads us out from ourselves. "Let us put the Holy Spirit back at the center of the Church," Francis said at Pentecost 2023, for "otherwise, our hearts will not be consumed by love for Jesus, but by love for ourselves." This has been his mission as pope. The aim of the dynamism he has given to the synod is to open the Church to the Spirit.

It is the Spirit that has always been the true protagonist in the Church, shaking it up and re-forming it, creating diversity and then forming it into a harmonious body. "The Holy Spirit always surprises us, to suggest fresh paths and new ways of speaking," as he put it at the Mass opening the synod on synodality in October 2021.

The Church was born at Pentecost in weakness, amidst hostility, and in the most improbable circumstances. There, in the tongues of fire and the gusts of wind, "all were filled" with the Holy Spirit, which led them to "go out from themselves" and "turned them into heralds of God's wondrous deeds" (EG 259).

Even today it is the Spirit that leads Christ's followers to spread consolation. It is the Spirit that equips ordinary people to proclaim the new life in God that Jesus has made possible by his life, death, and Resurrection. It is the Spirit that frees us from fear and excessive caution, impelling us to come out from what is safe and familiar, to go out to the margins. It is the Spirit that gives us gifts and charisms, and the power to speak of holy things and to be understood. It is the Spirit that allows us to tell of what we have seen and heard. It is the Spirit that gives us courage to live in a new way, in solidarity with the poor, in fraternal sharing, both captivating and scandalizing people by our freedom from what seems so important to this world, and by our love for those whom society despises and rejects. It is the Spirit that allows us to show what we have ourselves known: that life lived in the

Spirit and sharing in the life of God are not the privilege of the few but the right of all, available to all.

Within a short time after Pentecost, a very unlikely group of people spread the gospel to every country from Syria to Greece. It was the Spirit that made this possible, not least by its guidance in the very first synod, in chapter 15 of the Acts of the Apostles, which allowed the Christians to unshackle themselves from Jewish culture and customs and become truly global, incarnating the faith in every culture and language. Now another synod process under another Peter is seeking the guidance of the Spirit, to free the faith to enter our postmodern, globalized world and be born anew amidst the crises of our time.

In September 2023, as this book was moving through the editing stages, Francis undertook his most radically missionary trip yet, flying over nine hours eastward to the vast, landlocked, thinly populated nation of Mongolia, sandwiched between China and Russia. There he met with the country's Catholics, barely fourteen hundred of them, as well as some two hundred faithful who had come from China. He spoke to them in the cathedral of St. Peter and St. Paul, which had been built to look like a *ger*, Mongolia's traditional nomadic tent. At the end of his address, he reminded them that the kingdom of God is not born from great projects but in littleness. And he invited them to look to Mary, who showed that "being little is not a problem, but a resource."

As we end this retreat, and think about the places of our mission, our own Mongolias, we can imagine that Francis is addressing these words to us:

God loves littleness, and through it loves to accomplish great things, as Mary herself bears witness (Lk 1:48–49). Brothers and sisters, do not be concerned about small numbers, limited success, or apparent irrelevance. This is not how God works. Let us keep our gaze fixed on Mary, who in her littleness is greater than the heavens, for within her she bore the One whom the heavens and the highest heavens cannot contain (1 Kings 8:27). So let us entrust ourselves to her, asking for a renewed zeal and an ardent love that tirelessly and joyfully bears witness to the Gospel. Go forward! God loves you. He has chosen you and he believes in you. I am close to you, and I thank you most heartily. Thank you for your witness! Thank you for your lives poured out for the Gospel! Persevere, constant in prayer and creative in charity, steadfast in communion, joyful and meek in everything and with everyone. I bless you and keep you in my prayers. And I ask you, please, not to forget to pray for me.

SPIRITUAL EXERCISES, DAY 8 (WEEK 4)

Contemplation of the Resurrection (SE 219–229) and Contemplation to Attain Divine Love (SE 230–237)

- *Taking* the Resurrection narratives in Matthew (28:1–10), Mark (16:1–8), Luke (24:1–11), and John (John 20:11–18), as well as the story of Emmaus (Luke 24:13–35), imagine yourself there, coming to terms with the reality of the risen Christ. What are the stones of distrust and fear in you that need to be removed?
- *Read:* Very slowly, chapter 4 of *Christus Vivit*, asking for the grace "to be glad and rejoice intensely because of the great joy and the glory of Christ our Lord" (SE 221).
- *Read:* Part 3 of *Let Us Dream*. Thinking of your "belonging place," where, within this context, is your "Galilee," your "Mongolia"? How, in this context, are you called to exercise the "office of consoler" (SE 224)?

Contemplate-Discern-Propose

- *Contemplate:* Using the "Contemplation to Attain Divine Love," recall the blessings of creation and redemption and particular blessings in your life, including the particular gifts of this retreat.
- *Discern:* What fresh paths has the Spirit opened for you? What stops you?
- *Propose:* What next steps might you take now?

A User Guide

First Belong to God is written for any person or group of people drawn to know and follow Jesus more deeply, and who wants to do so through the teachings and wisdom of Francis. Using the Ignatian spiritual framework, which so deeply shaped him, it is intended as the basis of a retreat for "ordinary" disciples who desire and are able to take time out for reading, reflection, and prayer. It might, for example, be offered as a week's themed retreat by a spirituality center, or given to people in their homes over a much longer period, say, eight weeks, perhaps through a parish.

What matters is the desire to go deeper in the spiritual life, whether as individuals or together, as a community. That call may be felt especially against the background of the global synod on synodality (2021–24), which is calling on all believers to deepen communion, mission, and participation. Or it may be that, after ten years of the Francis pontificate, people desire to harvest and receive some of its many fruits.

Since first being given by St. Ignatius himself nearly five hundred years ago, the *Exercises* have been given in different ways in different contexts. In the classic or long form, retreatants withdraw from the world and keep silence for thirty days in the company of a spiritual director. The retreat is divided into four weeks, but each week is not seven days so much as it is a stage. In the First Week, you consider God's mercy and humankind's sin; in the Second, Jesus' incarnation and public ministry; in the Third, his Passion and death; and in the

Fourth, his Resurrection and continued life in the world. The classic, "long" retreat is done at most twice in a lifetime, and is particularly appropriate for people discerning their life's calling.

From very early on, the Jesuits also used the basic framework of the *Exercises* for eight-day "preached retreats" to groups and individuals unable to do the long retreat as well as people who wanted an annual "refresher" that allowed them to revisit the core meditations. This compressed form became popular in the nineteenth and twentieth centuries among religious congregations and laypeople. This eight-day preached retreat are the *Exercises* most people are familiar with today, especially in the Spanish-speaking world. Commonly, a group will go on retreat together, and a person is invited to give short talks each day, after which members of the group then go off to reflect on and pray in privacy. These talks are known as the "points," and they are usually tied to the theme or the exercises of that day.

First Belong to God offers those points for each of the eight days, in the form of four short texts that would be fifteen- to twenty-minute talks if given orally. But because it is a retreat "with Pope Francis," and intended as a way into his teachings, it has much more material for reading and reflection than is customary in an eight-day retreat. This risks making it too content-heavy and "heady." So if used in this way, a decision will need to be made about how best to allocate this reading: either in advance, or suggested for follow-up after.

Alternatively, the retreat could be given over a much longer period, as the basis of a course or cycle of talks in a parish or church organization, possibly tied to Lent or Advent. In this case, each "day" could offer the material for, say, a week's prayer and reflections at home, which would allow time to read the relevant chapters of encyclicals, etc. The retreatants might then gather once each week, in person or online, to share the fruits. If this were done synodally, using the method of conversation in the Spirit, it could help a parish or other kind of church body discern and deepen its mission.

At the end of each Day there are two kinds of prayer proposed. The first is tied specifically to the Ignatian meditation or contemplation of that day and is intended to be personal to each retreatant. The second, using the method of contemplate-discern-propose (or "see, judge, act" in its traditional formula), allows for a more free-flowing application of the fruits of the first prayer. If this is a group on retreat together, it could also be adapted for group faith-sharing. To help with planning and organizing a retreat using *First Belong to God*, an overview "map" of the retreat and its components follows.

Whether used in a retreat house, at home, or in a parish or other organization, *First Belong to God* is intended to facilitate what Francis calls the "primary encounter," that is, a direct experience of God's love and mercy, which leads to a choice and commitment. This retreat has been put together to help develop this capacity to discover and follow God's will, to recognize the signs of God's kingdom among us, and to commit to serving that kingdom in the place where we belong.

It is always advisable to discuss with an experienced spiritual director major questions or decisions that arise from prayer. As Francis says in *Let Us Dream*, it is always good to seek help from "people who are wise, who have been through the fire, people who can help you navigate what is to come."

Overview of the Retreat

DAY	TITLE	THEME OF THE DAY	SECTIONS	SPIRITUAL EXERCISES	TEXTS
ONE	Wonderfully Made	*On understanding ourselves as God-belonging creatures, made out of love for love*	I. Created in Love II. A Mission on This Earth III. Principle and Foundation IV. God Beholds Me	(Week 1) • *Principle and Foundation* (SE 23) • SE 46, 75	• *Laudato Si'*, chapter 2 • Psalms 17, 23, 34, 42, 63, and 131 • John 1:35–38 • Book of Tobit, chapter 11
TWO	To Come Out from Ourselves	*On the transforming power of God's mercy*	I. Encounter II. The Fall III. New Creation IV. Transfiguration	(Week 1) • *Meditation on sin and mercy* (SE 45–61)	• Genesis 2–4 • Parables of mercy in Luke 15 • *Misericordia et Misera* • *Evangelii Gaudium*, chapters 1 and 2
THREE	The Lord of the World	*On the lure of worldliness and how faith frees us from it*	I. Spiritual Worldliness II. The Lord of the World III. An *Examen* IV. To Live by Holiness	(Week 2) • *Meditation on worldliness* (SE 63) through an examen on my faith journey	• Chapter 1 of *Laudato Si'*, *Fratelli Tutti*, and/or *Let Us Dream*, in the light of Matthew 4:1–11 • *Evangelii Gaudium*, pp. 93–97; *Gaudete et Exsultate*, chapters 2 and 4 • Meeting Jesus: 1 John 2:12–17; John 1:43–51
FOUR	Called, Chosen, Sent	*On Jesus' call to work for his kingdom, and doing it his way*	I. I Hope in Him II. His Way III. God's Gaze IV. The Kingdom	(Week 2) • *The Call of the Good King* (SE 91–98) • Annunciation and Incarnation (SE 101–117)	• *Querida Amazonia*, chapter 1 ("social dream") • Beatitudes (Matthew 5:3–12; Luke 6:20–23) • *Gaudete et Exsultate*, chapter 3 • *Fratelli Tutti*, chapter 2 • Nativity and infancy (Matthew 1–2 and Luke 1–2) • "A day with Jesus": Mark 1:16–45

DAY	TITLE	THEME OF THE DAY	SECTIONS	SPIRITUAL EXERCISES	TEXTS
FIVE	The Ecology of Mercy	*On ourselves as creatures partnered with creation*	I. The Cry of the Earth II. A New Ark III. The Two Standards IV. A Time to Choose	(Week 2) • Meditation on the Two Standards (SE 136–148)	• *Querida Amazonia*, chapter 3 ("ecological dream") • *Laudato Si'*, chapter 4, especially 222–227 • *Let Us Dream*, pp. 30–35 • Prodigal Son (Luke 15:11–32)
SIX	Around the Common Table	*On the call to fraternity and to build a synodal Church*	I. Convocation in the Spirit II. Three Attachments III. Apostles of Fraternity IV. Thinking with the Church	(Week 2) • The Three Classes of Men (SE 149–157) • Rules for Discernment of Spirits (SE 328–336) and Thinking with the Church (SE 352–370)	• *Querida Amazonia*, chapter 2 ("social dream") • *Evangelii Gaudium*, 217–237 and *Fratelli Tutti*, chapters 4 and 6 • Catechees on discernment, 2022 • Conclusions of October 2023 synod • Mark 10:17–22; John, chapter 9
SEVEN	The Triumph of Failure	*On touching Christ's wounds, and the power of patience*	I. To Suffer With II. The Baited Hook III. Little Brother IV. Assuming Failure	(Week 3) • Contemplation of the Passion (SE 190–203)	• Gospel Passion narratives • Ibrahima Balde and Amets Arzallus Antia, *Little Brother: An Odyssey to Europe* • On Migration: *Evangelii Gaudium*, 210–211; *Laudato Si'*, 25; *Amoris Laetitia*, 46; *Gaudete et Exsultate*, 102–103
EIGHT	A New Imagination of the Possible	*On sharing Christ's joy and his peace in the Galilee of today*	I. The Consoler II. Galilee III. *Contemplatio* IV. To Go Out	(Week 4) • Contemplation of the Resurrection (SE 219–229) • Contemplation to Attain Divine Love (SE 230–237)	• Gospel Resurrection narratives • *Querida Amazonia*, chapter 4 ("ecclesial dream") • *Christus Vivit*, chapter 4 • *Laudato Si'*, 233–246 • *Desiderio Desideravi*, 44–46 • *Let Us Dream*, part 3

Leaving the Exercises

We might feel, at the conclusion of this retreat, something of what was in the heart of the apostle Peter on the Mount of Transfiguration: "Lord, it is good for us to be here!" (Matthew 17:4). Like Peter, we might want to try to hold on to the moment, freeze-frame it, build a tent. But of course, we can't; time is stronger than space. Retreats are followed by reentry into ordinary life. The question is, what will we take back into our daily existence?

When Francis asked that question at the concluding Mass of the week-long World Youth Day in Lisbon in August 2023, the answer he gave, taken from the Transfiguration, was threefold: to *shine*, to *listen*, and to *be unafraid*.

To *shine* (Matthew 17:2) meant "to love like Jesus: that is what makes us light," he told 1.5 million people in Tejo Park, adding, "Friends, I am telling you the truth: whenever you do works of love, you become light. But the moment you stop loving others and become self-centered, you extinguish your light."

To *listen* (Matthew 17:5) was to "listen to Jesus, for he will show you which paths are those of love. Listen to him."

To *be unafraid* was to hear what Jesus told his disciples on the Mount, and in so many other places in the Gospels: "Do not be afraid" (Matthew 17:7).

At the end of this retreat, it is good to think of the light and love we have received and how we can now reflect these back into our daily life. It is also good to listen carefully to what Jesus has said to us this week, and what paths we are now called to follow. We must also name our fears: that in returning to daily life, all this will be lost; that our dreams and plans will hit the hard rock of reality and dissipate; that we are inadequate to the task we feel called to perform.

These fears are a temptation to disbelieve the graces we have been given. They risk turning us back on ourselves, as if all depended on us, and in succumbing to them, we make them a reality. The most subtle distraction is perfectionism: that we cannot undertake something unless we will succeed. But in that way lies mediocrity, for we shut out grace. The prospect of failure for Christ's sake, one that allows God to act in the poverty of our means and possibilities, should never deter us. It is sometimes said that Jesus does not call the able, but enables those whom he calls. So "let us acknowledge our weakness, but allow Jesus to lay hold of it. . . . We are weak, yet we hold a treasure that can enlarge us and make those who receive it better and happier" (GE 131).

It is not our strength we depend on, but the Spirit's; we do not journey alone, but side by side with others in the Church (GE 141). Evangelization is never an isolated, individual act but always in and through the people of God, which is where our mission takes on concrete form. In the age of Francis, this means embracing synodal methods of communal discernment. Conversation in the Spirit is the means by which the fruits of this retreat can be shared with others, and lead to concrete actions.

Ignatius strongly urged people to continue the daily *examen* of conscience in their daily life, looking back each day using the five steps. It is also helpful as we leave the *Exercises* to do an *examen* on the retreat itself, to create a bridge between this experience and our daily lives. An *examen* allows us to review the retreat shortly after its end, either individually or as part of a group.

We might, for example, follow these five steps:

1. *What has been Good News for me this past week?* If I came with a particular desire or question, how has it been answered or clarified? What particular graces and wisdom have I been given? Pay attention in particular to unexpected gifts and surprises; Jesus goes before us. Were there particular moments of self-transcendence, when the Lord was taking me out of my shell? Was there a meditation or experience that brought a special illumination or clarity—of particular joy and peace, or excitement at new possibilities? In thanking God, we can also ask, Why might God have wanted to give me those gifts?

2. *What obstacles were revealed to me?* What particular weaknesses, tendencies or temptations have I discovered in myself or learned more about? What keeps me in my shell, holds me back from being the person I am created to be and from responding to the call Jesus makes to me? What have I learned this week about this tendency and how grace helps me deal with it, above all in Christ's Passion and Resurrection? What might I need to attend to in the future?

3. *What were the moments during this week when I felt unrest, darkness, and emptiness?* Desolation is an opportunity for growth. It is important to review these moments and ask God to help me to understand them. When desolation is followed by consolation or vice versa, it could be that the Lord is trying to teach me something. The turbulences of the "Week 2" contemplations about hearing Christ's call to me are especially important to review. Is there something here for which I may need to seek guidance?

4. *What decisions or commitments did I make in the course of this week?* This is the moment to review, in particular, the promises I made to Christ, or the resolutions I made. These need to be tested and confirmed. Which of them was the most important in the sense of the *magis?* Is there something I need now to examine and develop, to further pray over, perhaps to share with

others? One of the distinctive signs of a decision made in the good spirit is that it lasts over time; how can I put this commitment into practice and see if it is of God? It may be helpful to read *Gaudete et Exsultate* 147–157 on what it means to remain "in constant prayer."

5. *What is the Lord asking of me right now?* This might be as simple as making a resolution to pray more or to follow up on a prompt to do something in particular. This is the moment to jot down those prompts and decide to follow them through. This is also the moment to commit to what Francis calls *vigilance*. The graces we have received and the choices we have made can all too easily be lost because "we have not guarded our doors," as he warned in a catechesis on discernment. Keep watch over your heart, he said, because "vigilance is a sign of wisdom, but above all a sign of humility, because we are afraid to fall, and humility is the high road of Christian life." How can we "keep watch" over the fruits of this week in our hearts and humbly let them grow? (Chapter 5 of *Gaudete et Exsultate* may be helpful.)

In doing this *examen* prayerfully in the hours or days after our retreat, we will be aware of the extraordinary generosity and care with which the Lord treats us. But we may also become aware of why we decided to come on this retreat. It is demanding to go into the desert, not knowing what we will find, and offering ourselves for the Lord's service. Where did this generosity, this desire, come from? When we think back on this, we may find we were prompted—by something we saw or by what someone told us. Maybe the Spirit has reached us that way, and given us the courage to clear space for it.

So you see, all *is* gift. We *do* belong. And with that song in our hearts, as Francis likes to say, "Let's go ahead."

Sources

To avoid loading the text with footnotes, references that occur frequently are contained in the text itself; see Note on Acronyms in the front of the book. All other sources referred to are listed here.

Where no name is given, assume Pope Francis, whose homilies, speeches, encyclicals, etc. are all easily located at the Vatican website, vatican.va. To look up a reference, you need to know *the type of material it is*, e.g., homily, message, daily meditation, etc., as well as *the date,* both of which are given here. ("Address" and "Speech" are used interchangeably by the Vatican, but all are listed under "Speeches.")

The exception to this rule is if the speech, homily, etc. was part of an *apostolic journey,* in which case it will be listed at the Vatican website in a separate section, "Travels," which is divided into two: within and outside Italy. Here, what matters is to know both the *place* of the journey and its *date,* both of which have been given. Follow those links and you will find the item listed in the itinerary.

Where "Bergoglio" is mentioned instead of Francis, it refers to material that predates the pontificate (2013–), either from his years in the Society of Jesus (1959–1992) or as bishop and cardinal archbishop (1992–2013).

References to encyclicals and apostolic exhortations are by paragraph.

I have used Vatican English translations of papal texts wherever possible. However, in a few cases where there were none, I have made my own, and indicated this below. Wherever texts are cited from Bergoglio's Jesuit period, the translations are mine.

Introduction

- Pope Francis, Austen Ivereigh, *Let Us Dream: The Path to a Better Future* (New York: Simon & Schuster, 2020), 13–14.
- Pope Francis, *Gaudete et Exsultate: Apostalic Exhortation on the Call to Holiness in Today's World*, March 19, 2018.
- Homily, "Extraordinary Moment of Prayer" presided over by Pope Francis in the Sagrato of St. Peter's Basilica on March 27, 2020.
- On Jorge Mario Bergoglio as "storm pilot," see chapter 3 of my biography, *The Great Reformer: Francis and the Making of a Radical Pope* (New York: Pan MacMillan, 2015).
- Kim Samuel, *On Belonging: Finding Connection in an Age of Isolation* (New York: Abrams Press, 2022), xi.
- Zygmunt Bauman, *Liquid Modernity* (Cambridge: Polity Press, 2012), 162–3. On Francis and Bauman see Zeger Polhuijs, *Zygmunt Bauman and Pope Francis in Dialogue: The Labrynth of Liquid Modernity* (Lanham, Maryland: Rowman & Littlefield, 2022), chapter 4.
- General Audience, St. Peter's Square, September 27, 2023.

Day One: Wonderfully Made

Created in Love

- St. Ignatius of Loyola, as paraphrased by David L. Fleming, SJ.
- Thomas Merton, *Zen and the Birds of Appetite* (New York: New Directions, 1968).
- Dorothy Sayers, *The Mind of the Maker* (San Francisco: HarperCollins, 1968), 22.
- Makoto Fujimura, *Art and Faith: A Theology of Making* (New Haven, CT: Yale University Press, 2020), 7.
- Norman Wirzba, *Agrarian Spirit: Cultivating Faith, Community, and the Land* (Notre Dame, IN: Notre Dame University Press, 2022), 73.

A Mission on This Earth

- "Meeting with the Academic and Cultural World," Budapest, Hungary, April 30, 2023.
- Homily, Easter Vigil, April 8, 2023.

Principle and Foundation

- Jorge Mario Bergoglio, SJ, "Principio y Fundamento," in *Meditaciones para Religiosos* (Bilbao: Mensajero, 2014), 23.
- Angelus, Feast of the Assumption, August 15, 2023.
- Miguel Angel Fiorito, "Cristocentrismo del Principio y Fundamento de san Ignacio," 1961, in José Luis Narvaja, ed., *Miguel Angel Fiorito: Escritos*, vol II:1960–1970 (Rome: La Civiltà Cattolica, 2019), 48.

God Beholds Me

- Speech, Vigil of Pentecost, May 18, 2013.

- On St. Augustine on love and keeping the commandments, see Cardinal Bergoglio's speech "It is Possible to be Holy" in Pope Francis, *In Your Eyes I See My Words: Homilies and Speeches from Buenos Aires*, Volume 1:1999–2004, ed. Antonio Spadaro, trans. Marina A. Herrera (New York: Fordham University Press, 2019), 354–360.

- Homily, Holy Mass for World Youth Day, Parque Tejo, Lisbon, August 6, 2023.

Day Two: To Come Out from Ourselves

Encounter

- Arturo Sosa, SJ, *Walking with Ignatius*.

- On Cardinal Bergoglio's speech see chapter 9 of my *The Great Reformer*. In *Wounded Shepherd: Pope Francis and His Struggle to Convert the Catholic Church* (New York: Henry Holt, 2019), p. 159, I record his almost identical homily six years earlier at the Aparecida meeting. After hearing him both in 2007 and in 2013 many of the bishops and cardinals were convinced he had been "anointed" to lead the Church.

- *Salir de sí* is not always well rendered in the Vatican translations into English. Examples of its use are *Fratelli Tutti* 88, *Laudato Si'* 208, and *Gaudete et Exsultate* 131.

- St. Augustine's famous distinction is made in *De Civitate Dei* (The City of God), bk 14, c.28: *Fecerunt itaque civitates duas amores duo, terrenam scilicet amor sui usque ad contemptum Dei, caelestem vero amor Dei usque ad contemptum sui.*

- Homily, January 1, 2016.
- Pope Francis, Meeting on "The Protection of Minors in the Church," Address at the end of the Eucharistic Celebration, February 24, 2019.
- The first major interview was with Antonio Spadaro, SJ, published by *America* magazine as "A Big Heart Open to God," September 30, 2013.
- Miguel Angel Fiorito, SJ, *Cercare y Trovare La Volontà di Dio. Guida pratica agli Eercizi spirituali di sant'Ignazio di Loyola* (Milan: Ancora, 2021), 202.
- Story of the teenage Bergoglio's encounter with God's mercy in my *Wounded Shepherd*, 21–22.

The Fall

- Romano Guardini, *Power and Responsibility: A Course of Action for the New Age*, trans. Elinor C. Briefs (Chicago: Henry Regnery Co., 1961). Quotes here from first two chapters.
- On Bonhoeffer's use of *cor curvum in se* see Brian E. Gregor, *A Philosophical Anthropology of the Cross: The Cruciform Self* (Bloomington and Indianapolis, IN: Indiana University Press, 2013), 63.
- Dietrich Bonhoeffer, *Creation and Fall: A Theological Exposition of Genesis 1–3* (Minneapolis: Fortress Press, 2004). V. 6: "The Fall".
- Daily Meditation, "The devil exists," April 11, 2014.

New Creation

- Homily, Mass in Lampedusa, July 8, 2013.
- Fujimura, *Art and Faith*, esp. chapters 3 & 4.

Transfiguration

- Apostolic Journey to Chile: "Meeting with Priests, Consecrated Men and Women, and Seminarians," Cathedral of Santiago, January 16, 2018.
- Apostolic Letter, *Misericordia et Misera*, November 20, 2016, 16.
- Cardinal Bergoglio spoke of the woman caught in adultery in a 2012 retreat to Caritas described in *The Great Reformer*, ch. 8.

Day Three: The Lord of the World

Spiritual Worldliness

- Pope Francis, in conversation with the Jesuits of Chile and Peru (Lima, January 2018).
- Apostolic Journey to Sweden: "In-Flight Press Conference from Sweden to Rome," November 1, 2016, answer to Mathilde Imberty of Radio France.
- Henri de Lubac's warning and the phrase "spiritual worldliness" come in the final pages of his *Méditation Sur L'Eglise* (Paris: Cerf, 2003). In the English translation the warning comes on p. 378 of Henri de Lubac, *The Splendor of the Church*, trans. Michael Mason (San Francisco: Ignatius Press, 1999), 378.
- Homily, Mass with the new cardinals, February 15, 2015.
- Bergoglio, "La seducción del bienestar," in *Reflexiones sobre la Vida Apostólica* (Bilbao: Mensajero, 2013), 180–184. See also "El Espíritu del Mundo," in *Meditaciones para Religiosos* (Bilbao: Mensajero, 2013), pp. 147–149.
- Austen Ivereigh, "An Interview with Pope Francis," *Commonweal* magazine, May 2020 (available online).

The Lord of the World

- Robert Hugh Benson, *The Lord of the World* (London: Dodd, Mead & Co., 1907). The edition Bergoglio read was *El Señor del Mundo*, trans. Leonardo Castellani (Buenos Aires: Itinerarium, 1958). Helpful essay on the novel is by Aidan Nichols OP, "Imaginative Eschatology: Benson's 'The Lord of the World,'" *New Blackfriars*, January 1991, vol. 72, no. 845 (January 1991), 4–8.

- The Benson novel was referenced in a footnote to Pope Francis, Meeting on "The Protection of Minors in the Church," Address at the end of the Eucharistic Celebration, February 24, 2019. Among many other references are his comments to journalists on the flight from Manila (Apostolic Journey to the Philippines: In-Flight Press Conference, January 19, 2015) and his interviews with *Perfil* (March 13, 2023) and *La Nación* (March 20, 2023).

- Apostolic Journey to Hungary: Meeting with the Academic and Cultural World, April 30, 2023.

An Examen

- Jorge Mario Bergoglio, *En Él Solo La Esperanza: Ejercicios Espirituales a los Obispos Españoles, 15 al 22 de enero de 2006* (Madrid: BAC, 2013), ch. 4.

- Address to the Roman Curia, December 21, 2020. The idea that worldliness produces division in the apostolic body is a constant theme of his Jesuit talks on the subject.

- Apostolic journey to Rio de Janeiro: Address to the Leadership of the Episcopal Conferences of Latin America, July 28, 2013.

- Apostolic journey to Ecuador, Bolivia, and Paraguay: Holy Mass at Campo Grande, Asunción, July 12, 2015.

- Apostolic journey to Bangladesh: Press conference on the return flight from Bangladesh, December 2, 2017.

To Live by Holiness

- Address to the Roman Curia, December 21, 2020.
- Bergoglio, "Pecado y desperanza," in *Meditaciones* . . . p. 144.
- On Christ's resistance of Satan's temptations, see John G. Navone, *Triumph Through Failure: A Theology of the Cross* (Eugene, OR: Wipf and Stock), ch. 5.
- Morning meditation, "Frente a las tentaciones," May 8, 2018.

Day Four: Called, Chosen, Sent

Hope in Him

- Fernando Montes, SJ, *Amar y Servir a Cristo con Mirada Ignaciana: Síntesis de espiritualidad ignaciana.* Santiago de Chile: Ed. Univ. Alberto Hurtado, 2014, 27.
- Address, Third Edition of States General on Natality, May 12, 2023.
- Bergoglio, *En Él Solo La Esperanza: Ejercicios Espirituales a los Obispos Españoles*, 15 al 22 de enero de 2006. Madrid: Biblioetica de Autores Cristianos, 2013.

His Way

- On Jesus' ministry and proclamation, see See José Pagola, *Jesus: an Historical Approximation*, trans. Margaret Wilde (Miami: Convivium, 2009), esp. ch. 4.

God's Gaze

- On resonance—and the obstacles to it—see Hartmut Rosa, *Resonance: A Sociology of Our Relationship to the World*, trans. James C. Wagner (Cambridge, England: Polity Press, 2019).
- Austen Ivereigh, "An Interview with Pope Francis," *Commonweal*, May 2020.
- Apostolic journey to Marseille: Address, Final Session of the "Recontres Méditerranéenes," September 23, 2023.
- Apostolic journey to Mongolia: Meeting with charity workers, Ulaanbaatar, September 4, 2023.

The Kingdom

- Francis, interview with Belgian Catholic periodical *Tertio*, published in *L'Osservatore Romano*, February 28, 2023.
- Bishop Daniel E. Flores, "Closeness and the Common Journey: The role of synodality in a responsive Church," *Commonweal*, June 20, 2022.
- General Audiences on kingdom of God: March 6, 2019, and September 30, 2020.
- Apostolic journey to Morocco: Meeting with priests, religious, Cathedral of Rabat, March 31, 2019.
- Bergoglio, "La encarnación y el nacimiento" in *Meditaciones . . .* 239–43. Also, "El Señor, esperanza nuestra," in *Meditaciones . . .* 250–53.

Day Five: The Ecology of Mercy

The Cry of the Earth

- Brian Grogan, SJ, *Alone and on Foot: Ignatius of Loyola.*

- Wolf of Gubbio story from *The Little Flowers of Saint Francis*, trans. W. Heywood (London: Methuen & Co., 1906), ch. XXI.
- The story of St. Francis and Greccio is told in Brother Thomas of Celano, *The Life of St. Francis of Assisi*, trans. Catherine Bolton (Assisi: Ed Minerva, 2019), 169–70.
- Speech, visit to Assisi for the event "Economy of Francesco," September 24, 2022.
- Norman Wirzba, *This Sacred Life: Humanity's Place in a Wounded World* (Cambridge: Cambridge University Press, 2021), 154.
- *The Letter: Laudato Si' Film* can be watched for free on YouTube. For information and how to take action, see TheLetterFilm.org.

A New Ark

- On GDP as the core aim of Western economic policy, see chapter 1 of Kate Raworth, *Doughnut Economics: Seven Ways to Think Like a 21st-Century Economist* (London: Penguin Random House, 2017). Raworth, who is involved in the "Economy of Francesco" movement, is referred to by Francis in *Let Us Dream*, p. 64, where he also cites Mariana Mazzucato's *The Value of Everything: Making and Taking in the Global Economy* (London: Penguin Random House, 2019). Her quote is from p. 7. "What GDP measures and fails to measure and why" is discussed on pp. 75–100.
- Gaël Giraud, SJ, "The Real Obstacles to Ecological Transition," *La Civiltà Cattolica* in English, March 27, 2023, available online.
- Apostolic journey to Canada: Homily, Lac Ste. Anne, July 26, 2022.

The Two Standards

- Francis quoted from Ibrahima Balde and Amets Arzallus Antia, *Little Brother: An Odyssey to Europe*, trans. Timberlake Wertenbaker (London: Scribe Publications, 2021). The book is discussed again on Day 7.

- On René Girard's "mimetic desire," see a recent introduction to his insights: Luke Burgis, *Wanting: The Power of Mimetic Desire in Everyday Life* (St. Martin's Press/Swift Press, 2021).

- On Bernardone's conversion, see Brother Thomas of Celano, *The Life of St. Francis of Assisi*, ch. 1.

- Giraud in Gaël Giraud and Carlo Petrini, *Il Gusto di Cambiare: La Transizione Ecologica come Via per la Felicità* (Rome: LEV/ Slow Food Editore, 2023), 166.

Day Six: Around the Common Table

Convocation in the Spirit

- St. Ignatius on the deliberations of the Jesuits in 1539 in Rome.

- Audience with the Delegation for the presentation of the "È Giornalismo" Prize, August 26, 2023.

- Speech commemorating the 50th anniversary of the institution of the Synod of Bishops, October 17, 2015.

- Speech, "First Greeting of the Holy Father, Pope Francis," March 13, 2013.

- Francis homilies at opening and conclusion of synod assembly, October 4 & October 29, 2023.

- Francis address opening the synod, October 4, 2023.

- Cardinal Jean-Claude Hollerich, "Relazione introduttiva," October 4, 2023, at synod.va.

- "A Synodal Church in Mission." Synthesis Report of the XVI Ordinary General Assembly of the Synod of Bishops: First Session, Oct 4–29, 2023, at synod.va.
- Apostolic Journey to Chile: Meeting with Priests, Consecrated Men and Women, and Seminarians, Cathedral of Santiago, January 16, 2018.

Three Attachments

- Bergoglio's talks are "Tres binarios" in *Meditaciones* . . . 173–8, "Acerca del Magis" in *Reflexiones Espirituales* 55–94, and *En Él Solo La Esperanza*, ch. 9.
- On the *magis* see Barton T. Geger, SJ, "What Magis Really Means and Why It Matters," in *Jesuit Higher Education* 1(2): 16–31 (2012).
- This reading of the man born blind through the lens of the Three Kinds of Men comes from Fiorito, *Cercare e Trovare*, 521–525.

Apostles of Fraternity

- Analysis of the social media environment is in the Vatican's Dicastery for Communications 2023 document, "Towards Full Presence: A Pastoral Reflection on Engagement with Social Media," at vatican.va.
- *Instrumentum Laboris* for the First Session (October 2023) of the XVI Ordinary General Assembly of the Synod of Bishops, B 1.1(d).
- "Ideas can be discussed . . .": among many examples of his use of this dictum is his Letter to the bishops of the United States Conference of Catholic Bishops, January 1, 2019.
- Apostolic journey to the United States: Address, visit to the Joint Session of the US Congress, September 24, 2015.

- Homily, July 23, 2023.

- On communicating in a context of polarization, see Diego
  Fares, SJ, and Austen Ivereigh, "How to communicate in a
  polarized society," *La Civiltà Cattolica*, En. Ed., vol. 3, no. 3,
  article 5, March 2019.

- For a detailed account of the Viganò episode see my *Wounded
  Shepherd*, 136–144, which has quotes from Francis's morning
  homilies.

- Francis summarizes his lessons from Guardini on
  contrapositions versus contradictions in *Let Us Dream*, 78–81.
  More detail in Massimo Borghesi, *The Mind of Pope Francis:
  Jorge Mario Bergoglio's Intellectual Journey* (Collegeville, MN:
  Liturgical Press, 2018), chapter 3. See also Bergoglio, "Fin de
  año," in *Reflexiones Espirituales*, 166, and "Necesidad de una
  antropología politica: un problema pastoral," in *Reflexiones en
  Esperanza* (Rome: LEV/Romana, 2013), 261.

- On Ignatius not fearing disagreement: Bergoglio, "La
  consolación: ámbito de la unión de los ánimos," in *Reflexiones en
  Esperanza*, 232.

Thinking with the Church

- Address, "Ceremony commemorating the 50th anniversary of
  the institution of the synod of bishops," October 17, 2015. This
  and his other many addresses on synodality are collected in Pope
  Francis, *Walking Together: The Way of Synodality* (Maryknoll,
  NY: Orbis Books, 2023).

- Address to members of the National Council of Italian Catholic
  Action, April 30, 2021.

- On "conversation in the Spirit" see section A2 of the October 23 Synod's working document, the *Instrumentum Laboris*, at synod.va.
- On attitudes and mindsets needed for synodality, see the International Theological Commission's "Synodality in the Life and Mission of the Church," esp. chapter 4, at vatican.va.
- On Ignatius's Rules for Thinking with the Church and their application to the synod, see Paul Rolphy Pinto, SJ, "A Spirituality of Synodality in the Spiritual Exercises," *Ignaziana* 34 (2022): 123–134.
- Bergoglio, "Sentido Eclesial," *Meditaciones*, 111–115.
- Speech to the 36th General Congregation of the Society of Jesus, October 24, 2016.

Day Seven: The Triumph of Failure

To Suffer With

- Pope Francis, address to General Congregation 36 of the Society of Jesus in Rome, 2016.
- On Ignatius's "apostolic purpose" in the Third Week, see Fiorito, *Cercare e Trovare*, 797–799.
- Pope's prayer intention for September 2023, "For people living on the margins," is at popesprayerusa.net.
- Homily, Palm Sunday, April 5, 2020.
- Apostolic letter *Desiderio Desideravi: on the Liturgical Formation of the People of God*, June 29, 2022.

The Baited Hook

- Bergoglio, "Silencio y Palabra," in *Reflexiones en Esperanza*, 115–153. Although he does not reference René Girard, the references in both Bergoglio and Girard to Maximus the

Confessor's image of the hook and the poisoned bait as well as the shared references to the scapegoat mechanism are very striking.

- Girard quotes here from René Girard, *I See Satan Fall Like Lightning*, trans. James G. Williams (Maryknoll, NY: Orbis Books, 2001), esp. chapter 11, "The Triumph of the Cross."

Little Brother

- Ibrahima Balde and Amets Arzallus Antia, *Little Brother: An odyssey to Europe*. Francis spoke about the book in conversation with the Jesuits ("What is the Church's Vocation? Pope Francis in conversation with the Maltese Jesuits," *La Civiltà Cattolica*, English edition, April 15, 2022) and in an address to a delegation from Caritas Spain, September 5, 2022.
- Apostolic journey to Lampedusa: Homily, July 8, 2013.
- On Francis and migration, see Austen Ivereigh, "Why does Pope Francis focus on migration? Because God asks for mercy, not sacrifice," *Commonweal*, March 11, 2023.
- On treating migration as a national security issue and the Texas reports, see articles by Kevin Clarke: "Will Europe change course on migration?," *America* magazine, June 28, 2023, and "'Push the people back into the water.' Texas bishops condemn inhumane border policies after leaked email," *America* magazine, July 20, 2023.
- Apostolic journey to Mexico: Homily, Ciudad Juárez, February 17, 2016.
- Apostolic journey to Cyprus and Greece: Ecumenical prayer with migrants, Nicosia, December 3, 2021; Address, Reception and Identification Centre in Mytilene, Lesbos, December 5, 2021.

- Letter to Archbishop Alessandro of Agrigento on occasion of the tenth anniversary of the visit to Lampedusa, June 20, 2023.

Assuming Failure

- Bergoglio, "Nuestra carne en oración" and "La carne sacerdotal de Cristo," in *Reflexiones en Esperanza*, 13–68.
- I discuss Navone's influence on Bergoglio in *Wounded Shepherd*, 78–80. Navone himself discusses Francis's appreciation of his work in an afterword to a 2014 reprint of his *Triumph through Failure: A Theology of the Cross* (Eugene, Oregon: Wipf & Stock, 2014), from which these quotes come. The original edition was by Paulist Press in New York in 1974.
- Karl Rahner, *Spiritual Exercises* (London: Sheed & Ward, 1956), 224–5.
- Homily, "Extraordinary Moment of Prayer" presided over by Pope Francis in the Sagrato of St. Peter's Basilica on March 27, 2020.
- Cardinal José Tolentino Mendonça's retreat is published in English as *Thirst: our Desire for God, God's Desire for Us*, trans. Demetrio S. Yocum (New York: Paulist Press, 2019), 72.
- Apostolic journey to the United States: Meeting with the bishops of the USA, Washington, DC, September 23, 2015.

Day Eight: A New Imagination of the Possible

The Consoler

- Pope Francis, *Christus Vivit* (2018), 126.
- Bergoglio's retreat talks on the Resurrection are: "La Paz" and "El Señor, muerte y resurrección nuestra" in *Meditaciones* . . . 193–5, 254–7.

- "A Plan to Rise Again" in Pope Francis, *Life After the Pandemic*, preface by Card. Michael Czerny, SJ (Rome: Libreria Editrice Vaticana, 2020), 43–44. (Originally "Un plan para resucitar: una meditación," *Vida Nueva*, April 17, 2020.)
- Homily, Pentecost, June 9, 2019.
- Homily, Easter Vigil, April 20, 2019.

Galilee

- Easter Vigil homilies since 2020 on Galilee: April 11, 2020; April 3, 2021; April 8, 2023.
- Address to the Roman Curia, December 21, 2019.
- Tomáš Halík, *Pomeriggio del Cristianesimo: Il Coraggio di Cambiare* (Milan: Vita e Pensiero, 2022), ch. 16. My translations.
- For a summary of Hálik's thinking, see José Frazão Correia, SJ, "What Form Will Future Christianity Take?," *La Civiltà Cattolica* in English, March 22, 2023.
- Tomas Halik's "Spiritual Introduction" to the European synodal continental assembly, Prague, is on YouTube.
- Bergoglio, "En El Solo Poner la Esperanza," *Reflexiones en Esperanza*, 254.

Contemplatio

- Bergoglio's retreat talks on or referring to the *contemplatio*: "La Memoria" in *Meditaciones*, 196–200; "Epifanía y Vida" in *Reflexiones en esperanza*, 78; *En Él Solo La Esperanza*, 113–128.
- Commentary on the *contemplatio* in Fiorito, *Cercare e Trovare*, 943–964.

- "A Francisco de Borja, Duque de Gandía," Rome, 1545 (Epp 1, 339–342), in Ignacio de Loyola, *Cartas Esenciales, introducción y edición de Manuel Ruiz Jurado SJ* (Bilbao: ed. Mensajero, 2017), n. 17. (Author's translation.)
- Apostolic Letter, "Desiderio Desideravi: on the Liturgical Formation of the People of God," June 29, 2022.

To Go Out

- Dialogue with the Jesuits in Peru, "Where have our people been creative?," *La Civiltà Cattolica* in English, February 15, 2018.
- Homily, Pentecost, May 19, 2013.
- Apostolic Exhortation *Christus Vivit: to Young People and to the entire People of God*, Mach 25, 2019.
- Catechesis on evangelization: quotes are from the General Audiences of January 11, 2023 and February 22, 2023.
- Homily, Pentecost, May 28, 2023.
- Homily, Opening of the synodal path, October 10, 2021.
- Pentecost homilies: June 9, 2019; May 31, 2020; May 23, 2021; and May 28, 2023.
- Apostolic journey to Mongolia: Meeting with bishops, priests, missionaries (etc.), cathedral of SS Peter and Paul, Ulaanbaatar, September 2, 2023.

Leaving the Exercises

- Apostolic journey to Portugal for XXXVII World Youth Day: Homily, Mass, Parque Tejo, Lisbon, August 6, 2023.
- General Audience, December 14, 2022. Catechesis on Discernment, 12: Vigilance.

Bibliography

Balde, Ibrahima and Amets Arzallus Antia. *Little Brother: An Odyssey to Europe.* Trans. Timberlake Wertenbaker. London: Scribe, 2021.

Balthasar, Hans Urs von. "On Vicarious Representation." In *Explorations in Theology IV: Spirit and Institution.* San Francisco: Ignatius Press, 1995.

Bauman, Zygmunt. *Liquid Modernity.* Cambridge: Polity Press, 2012.

Benson, Robert Hugh. *The Lord of the World.* London: Dodd, Mead & Co., 1907.

Bonhoeffer, Dietrich. *Creation and Fall: A Theological Exposition of Genesis 1–3.* Minneapolis: Fortress Press, 2004.

Borghesi, Massimo. *The Mind of Pope Francis: Jorge Mario Bergoglio's Intellectual Journey.* Collegeville, MN: Liturgical Press, 2018.

Burgis, Luke. *Wanting: The Power of Mimetic Desire, and How to Want What You Need.* St. Martin's Press/Swift Press, 2021.

De Lubac, Henri. *The Splendor of the Church.* Trans. Michael Mason. San Francisco: Ignatius Press, 1999.

Fares, Diego, SJ. "La fratellanza umana. Il suo valore transcendentale e programmatico nell'itinerario di papa Francesco," *La Civiltà Cattolica* 2019 III: 20 July/3 August 2019 114–126 n. 4058.

Fares, Diego, SJ, and Austen Ivereigh. "How to communicate in a polarized society." *La Civiltà Cattolica,* English Edition, vol. 3, no. 3, article 5, March 2019.

Fiorito, Miguel Angel, SJ. *Cercare y Trovare La Volontà di Dio. Guida pratica agli Eercizi spirituali di sant'Ignazio di Loyola*. Milan: Ancora, 2021.

Francis (Pope) / Jorge Mario Bergoglio. *En Él Solo La Esperanza: Ejercicios Espirituales a los Obispos Españoles, 15 al 22 de enero de 2006*. Madrid: BAC, 2013.

_____. Spadaro, Antonio. *In Your Eyes I See My Words: Homilies and Speeches from Buenos Aires*, Volume 1:1999–2004; Volume 2:2005–2008. (ed.), trans. Marina A. Herrera. New York: Fordham University Press, 1999, 2020.

_____. *Let Us Dream: The Path to a Better Future. In conversation with Austen Ivereigh*. New York: Simon & Schuster, 2020.

_____. *Life After the Pandemic*. Preface by Card. Michael Czerny, SJ. Rome: Libreria Editrice Vaticana, 2020.

_____. *Meditaciones para Religiosos*. Bilbao: Mensajero, 2014.

_____. *Reflexiones sobre la Vida Apostólica*. Bilbao: Mensajero, 2013.

_____. *Reflexiones en Esperanza*. Rome: LEV/Romana, 2013.

_____. *Walking Together: The Way of Synodality*. Maryknoll, NY: Orbis Books, 2023.

Francis (Saint). *The Little Flowers of Saint Francis*. Trans. W. Heywood. London: Methuen & Co., 1906.

Frazão Correia, José, SJ. "What Form Will Future Christianity Take?" *La Civiltà Cattolica* in English (March 22, 2023).

Fujimura, Makoto. *Art and Faith: A Theology of Making*. New Haven, CT: Yale University Press, 2020.

Geger, Barton T., SJ. "What Magis Really Means and Why It Matters," in *Jesuit Higher Education* (2012) 1(2): 16–31.

Girard, René. *I See Satan Fall Like Lightning*. Ossining, NY: Orbis Books, 2001.

Girard, René. *I See Satan Fall Like Lightning*. Trans. James G. Williams. Maryknoll, NY: Orbis Books, 2001.

Giraud, Gaël, SJ, and Carlo Petrini. *Il Gusto di Cambiare: La Transizione Ecologica come Via per la Felicità*. Rome: LEV/Slow Food Editore, 2023.

Giraud, Gaël, SJ, and Erika Guadalupe Ruiz Lara. "The Real Obstacles to Ecological Transition." *La Civiltá Cattolica* (March 27, 2023).

Gregor, Brian E. *A Philosophical Anthropology of the Cross: The Cruciform Self*. Bloomington and Indianapolis, IN: Indiana University Press, 2013.

Grogan, Brian, SJ. *Alone and on Foot: Ignatius of Loyola*. Dublin: Veritas, 2008.

Guardini, Romano. *Power and Responsibility: A Course of Action for the New Age*. Trans. Elinor C. Briefs. Chicago: Henry Regnery Co., 1961.

Halík, Tomáš. *The Afternoon of Christianity: The Courage to Change*. Trans. Gerald Turner. Notre Dame, IN: University of Notre Dame Press, 2024. [*Pomeriggio del Cristianesimo: Il Coraggio di Cambiare*. Milan: Vita e Pensiero, 2022.]

Ignatius of Loyola. *The Spiritual Exercises of St. Ignatius*. Trans. Louis J. Puhl. New York: Vintage Spiritual Classics/Random House, 2000.

_____. *Cartas Esenciales, introducción y edición de Manuel Ruiz Jurado SJ*. Bilbao: Mensajero, 2017.

Ivereigh, *The Great Reformer: Francis and the Making of a Radical Pope*. New York: Pan MacMillan, 2015.

_____. *Wounded Shepherd: Pope Francis and His Struggle to Convert the Catholic Church*. New York: Henry Holt, 2019.

Mazzucatto, Mariana. *The Value of Everything: Making and Taking in the Global Economy*. London: Penguin Random House, 2019.

Merton, Thomas. *Zen and the Birds of Appetite*. New York: New Directions, 1968.

Narvaja, José Luis, ed. *Miguel Angel Fiorito: Escritos, vol II: 1960–1970*. Rome: La Civiltà Cattolica, 2019.

Navone, John J., SJ. *Triumph through Failure: A Theology of the Cross*. Eugene, OR: Wipf and Stock, 2014.

Pagola, José. *Jesus: An Historical Approximation*. Trans. Margaret Wilde. Miami: Convivium, 2009.

Polhuijs, Zeger. *Zygmunt Bauman and Pope Francis in Dialogue: The Labrynth of Liquid Modernity*. Lanham, Maryland: Rowman & Littlefield, 2022.

Rahner, Karl, SJ. *Spiritual Exercises*. London: Sheed & Ward, 1956.

Raworth, Kate. *Doughnut Economics: Seven Ways to Think Like a 21st-Century Economist*. London: Penguin Random House, 2017.

Rolphy Pinto, Paul, SJ. "A Spirituality of Synodality in the Spiritual Exercises." *Ignaziana* 34 (2022): 123–134.

Rosa, Hartmut. *Resonance: A Sociology of Our Relationship to the World*. Trans. James C. Wagner. Cambridge: Polity Press, 2019.

Samuel, Kim. *On Belonging: Finding Connection in an Age of Isolation*. New York: Harry N. Abrams, 2022.

Sosa, Arturo, SJ. *Walking with Ignatius*. Dublin: Messenger Publications, 2021.

Thomas, Brother (of Celano). *The Life of St. Francis of Assisi*. Trans. Catherine Bolton. Assisi: Ed Minerva, 2019.

Tolentino Mendonça, José. *Thirst: Our Desire for God, God's Desire for Us*. Trans. Demetrio S. Yocum. New York: Paulist Press, 2019.

Wirzba, Norman. *Agrarian Spirit: Cultivating Faith, Community, and the Land*. Notre Dame, IN: Notre Dame University Press, 2022.

_____. *This Sacred Life: Humanity's Place in a Wounded World*. Cambridge: Cambridge University Press, 2021.

Acknowledgments

First Belong to God is dedicated to the memory of Fr. Diego Fares, SJ (1955–2022), an Argentine Jesuit who understood Pope Francis and his heart and mind better than anyone else. From 2015 to his early death in 2022 he was one of the writers at *La Civiltà Cattolica* in Rome, where I used to visit him in search of advice and guidance. We became friends, and I missed him greatly in the writing of this book. He has influenced it in many important ways. I hope he would be pleased with it.

I would like to thank many Jesuit and other spiritual directors who over the years and in different countries have patiently guided me through the *Spiritual Exercises*. In particular I want to mention Paddy Purnell, SJ, and Ian Tomlinson, SJ, both at St. Beuno's in Wales; Antonio Allende, SJ, in Loyola, Spain; Rafael Velasco, SJ, in Buenos Aires; and in Santiago de Chile, Fernando Montes, SJ. This text has also benefitted in many ways from their insights and inputs.

Special thanks are due to Damian Howard, SJ, and Leonard Moloney, SJ, the British and Irish provincials at the time of the original 2020 retreat. Damian asked me to give it, ignoring my protestations of unworthiness, and urged me afterwards to publish it; Leonard, shocked in 2022 I hadn't done so, opened some doors to enable me to make it happen. Thanks, too, to Ruth Holgate, the director of St. Beuno's, for helping me put together the original retreat in the weird time of lockdown.

Gary Jansen and his editing team at Loyola Press have been wonderful to work with, improving the text in so many ways. Thanks, as ever, to my agent, Bill Barry. My wife, Linda, has lovingly kept the show on the road, enabling the belonging on which creativity depends.

Finally, heartfelt thanks to Pope Francis, not just for the foreword, but for his countless gestures of kindness and encouragement and endless good humor. (When I told him I was writing a book subtitled *On Retreat with Pope Francis* he joshed, "Really? And what does the pope say about it?") In his guidance of the church and humanity these past ten years, we couldn't have asked for a greater spiritual director.

About the Author

Austen Ivereigh is a UK-based writer and commentator known for his books written about and with Pope Francis. A Fellow in contemporary Church history at Campion Hall, Oxford, he regularly contributes to *The Tablet* and *America*, and is a sought-after speaker and retreat-giver. He is the author of two authoritative biographies of Pope Francis, *The Great Reformer* (2014) and *Wounded Shepherd* (2019). In 2020 he co-authored with Pope Francis the *New York Times* bestseller *Let Us Dream: The Path to a Better Future*.

MORE BOOKS ABOUT **IGNATIAN SPIRITUALITY**

What Is Ignatian Spirituality?
Experiencing the Spiritual Exercises
of St. Ignatius in Daily Life

DAVID L. FLEMING, SJ

In *What Is Ignatian Spirituality?* David L. Fleming, SJ, provides an authoritative yet highly accessible summary of the key elements of Ignatian spirituality, among which are contemplative prayer, discernment, and dynamic involvement in service and mission.

In twenty concise chapters, Fr. Fleming explains how this centuries-old method of disciplined reflection on God's work in the world can deepen our spiritual lives today and guide all the decisions we make.

English: Paperback | 978-0-8294-2718-9 | $12.99
Spanish: Paperback | 978-0-8294-3883-3 | $12.95

Ignatian Spirituality A to Z

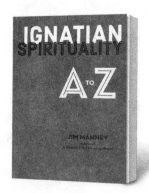

JIM MANNEY

With *Ignatian Spirituality A to Z*, Jim Manney has developed a brief, informative, and entertaining guide to key concepts of Ignatian spirituality and essential characters and events in Jesuit history. From Pedro Arrupe to Francis Xavier, from Ad Majorem Dei Gloriam to Zeal, this book uncovers the rich language of the Jesuits. It will be an indispensable tool to anyone interested in Ignatian spirituality, to staff, faculty, and students at Jesuit institutions and schools, and to clergy and spiritual directors who advise others about prayer and spiritual matters.

Paperback | 978-0-8294-4598-5 | $14.95